HEALTHY VENEZUELAN COOKING

BY THE NOMAD COOK
PHOTOGRAPHY BY THE NOMAD COOK

Published by The Nomad Cook
Printed by Create Space
Copyright © 2014 The Nomad Cook
All rights reserved

ISBN: 1500441317

ISBN-13: 978-1500441319

This cookbook is dedicated to all the foodies out there who enjoy cooking and exploring new healthy recipes

Contents

page

Introduction 9

Beef 17
Beef in Tomato Sauce 18
Churrasco 20
Coconut Goat Stew 22
Goat Tarkari 24
Ground Beef 26
Parrilla 28
Shredded Beef (v) 30
Skirt Steak 32

Chicken 35
Chicken and Potatoes 36
ChickenCroquettes 38
Chicken Provenzal 40
Shredded Chicken (v) 42

Drinks 45
3 in 1 juice 46
Aloe Vera juice 48
Papaya juice 50
Papelon con Limon 52
Pineapple Cocada 54
Pumpkin juice 56
Sesamejuice 58
Tizana 60
Watermelon and Pineapplejuice 62

Fish and Seafood........... 65
Baked Snapper... 66
Broiled Mahi mahi in Adobo rub................... 68
Calamari Stew... 70
Pan-fried Whole Grouper.............................. 72
Rompe Colchon.. 74
Seafood Casserole....................................... 76
Venezuelan style Bacalao............................. 78

Rice........... 81
Arroz con Pollo (v)...................................... 82
Rice with Shrimp... 84
Seafood Soupy rice..................................... 86
White rice (v).. 88

Salads........... 91
Avocado and Shrimp salad (v)..................... 92
Beets and Potato salad (v)........................... 94
Cabbage salad (v)....................................... 96
Criolla salad (v).. 98
Hen salad (v).. 100
Russian salad (v)...................................... 102

Sauces........... 105
Garlic sauce (v)... 106
German sauce (v)...................................... 108
Green sauce (v).. 110
Guasacaca (v)... 112
Picante Pickled sauce (v)........................... 114
Pink sauce (v)... 116
Sofrito (v)... 118
Venezuelan Criolla sauce (v)...................... 120

Soups.. 123
Asparagus Cream soup (v)... 124
Avocado Cream soup (v)... 126
Fosforera.. 128
Green Plantain soup (v)... 130
Milk soup (v)... 132
Oriental Red Snapper soup... 134
Pisca Andina (v).. 136
Pumpkin soup (v).. 138
Sancocho (v)... 140

Spreads, Fillings and Dips..................... 143
Caraotas (v).. 144
Cazon... 146
Chicken LiverPate... 148
Mashed Avocado (v)... 150
Perico (v).. 152
Reina Pepiada (v).. 154
Sardines and Tomato dip... 156
Tomatada (v).. 158
Tuna filling... 160

Street Food.. 163
Hot Dogs (v)... 164
Patacones (v).. 166
Peanut Hamburgers... 168
Pepito sandwhich.. 170

Venezuelan Staples.. 173
Arepas (v).. 174
Cachapas (v).. 176
Empanadas (v)... 178
Ham Bread... 180
Pabellon (v).. 182
Tajadas(v).. 184
Tostones (v)... 186

Resources.. 189

Introduction

Venezuela is located on the Northern coast of South America. The cuisine reflects its biodiversity and multi-cultures coexisting with one another, making it one of the most varied in the region. There is a strong Mediterranean influence given the wide variety of migration from Spain, France, Italy and Portugal as well as African (through populations of slaves brought by the Spaniards) Caribbean, Hindi, plus Indigenous who already occupied the territory.

It is known for the extended use of corn/maize, plantains, peppers, grains, beans, root vegetables, sugar cane, meats and different varieties of birds, from which many dishes with unique and extraordinary flavors come from. Among these delectable dishes are Pabellon Criollo, Arepas, Empanadas, Cachapas, Pisca Andina, Tarkari de Chivo and Sancocho, which are included in detail in this cookbook.

Due to the territorial extension and the diversity of agricultural resources, Venezuelan cuisine varies by region and the typical elements of the food of each region are as follows:

*East, Guyana and the Caribbean: predominance of wild-caught sea water and river fish, seafood and lobsters. Root crops like yams, yuca and potatoes. Beef in the south-plains area where there's production of soft fresh cheeses such as Guayanes, Hand, Braided, Mozzarella Criolla, etc. Everyday meals are fried or stewed fish served with arepas, rice, salad and sweet plantains or tostones. And there are tendencies of European dishes such as clams in white wine sauce, paella, etc.

*West and Zulia: consumption of goat, lamb, and rabbit. Tendencies to local dishes with large Indigenous and European influences. There's also a variety of fast foods particularly from the Zulia state, among these are: Patacon, Tumbarrancho (a variety of arepas), and fried wheat pies.

*Central: more diversity of food by being closer to productive areas, but a lack of major agriculture regions make for large consumption of chicken, pork, beef, fish stews or roasts, rice, pasta, salads and a big influence of international cuisines ranging from Spanish, Italian, French, Portuguese and other European countries such as Germany, etc.

*Plains: similar cuisine to the plains from Brazil, Uruguay and Argentina. Large consumption of beef and game such as Chiguire, Lapa and Morrocoy. Grilled, roasted and meat on a stick served with cachapas. High production of cheese and milk derivatives.

*Andes: related to the Colombian Andes; use of potatoes, wheat and root crops. Beef, lamb, chicken, very little consumption of fish except for farmed trout. European oriented and stays true to the South American Andes' cuisine.

History and Origins

Aboriginal people began to develop their diet similar to the Paleolithic, by what they found in nature; through hunting, fishing and farming, but some of their preparations were not simple. The nutritious regime of the Venezuelan native was based on corn and yuca (cassava), supplemented with animal protein and a natural sweetener, honey. Fat was not included in culinary preparations and the quintessential seasoning was the pepper. Most of the tribes depended on fishing, hunting and gathering, therefore habits of eating at a certain time were nonexistent.

Aware of fire, Indigenous people had learned to cook by placing their food on wooden grills or fired mud griddles and even burying them wrapped in leaves (barbecue). Some chronicles indicate they made their own clay pots by hand.

Their recipe range was restrictive but not as simple as many believe. Maize (zea mayst), essential in native food, was rigged in various ways. The Arepa had a series of previous preparations which began by de-kernelling the cobs once dry, then boiling and grinding until obtaining a dough from which small cakes were ensemble and cooked on a mud griddle. For chicha (rice drink), besides hulling, there was a fermentation time and grinding, often times done by women.

Arrival of the Spaniards meant the inevitable exchange of cultures and in this encounter with natives they had a direct contact with their foods which they gradually introduced into their diets. Spaniards brought new products from their travels. Among them were olive oils, barley, wine, wheat, spices (bay leaves, saffron, oregano, rosemary, etc.) and other foods like figs, cabbage, fava beans and pomegranates. Salt was widely used in food preparations by the Spaniards and cooking tools were made of iron, glass, silver, wood and fired clay.

Spaniards didn't come to America alone, they brought slaves from Africa, who had similar costumes as the American aborigines, with simple lifestyles. They consumed very little salt, but used black pepper and ginger as a spice in abundance. There were predominant uses of vegetable fats in their diet: palm oil and a vegetable margarine made from a plant named " Karite " were commonly used and sesame oil in small amounts. Their utensils were wooden containers, mortars, and spoons, clay pots and iron knives.

In the mid 1800's, Venezuelan cuisine began a refinement as a result of the arrivals of Italians, Portuguese, Turks, Greeks, Syrians and the rest of the Mediterranean basin who left a series of contributions with ingredients and ways of cooking. And then continued in the 1950's with European and Latin American migration which would be a big influence too.

Later on, with the oil boom in the 1970's, French and Italians were the ones giving a cosmopolitan touch to Venezuelan cuisine in Caracas, the capital. They and other migratory flows, such as Chinese, Jewish, Arab, German, Caribbean, Colombian, Peruvian, Ecuadorian, Mexican and large U.S. fast food chains, along with the efforts of Venezuelans (which derive from the synthesis of the contributions of Natives and Africans), their determination and diversity created what is known today as Venezuelan gastronomy.

The New Healthy Venezuelan Cooking

Venezuelan food is made from scratch with fresh ingredients and sometimes it may even be organic. However, there are still unhealthy tendencies which need to be addressed and changed to make it healthier and more nutritious. Latinos and Latin food cooks, in general, are still using unhealthy oils, sugars, processed spices with harmful chemicals and practicing unhealthy ways of cooking which may be the reason for many illnesses. They may not know this yet as there is miscommunication around this topic. Here are healthier alternatives and changes I have made in this cookbook:

Unhealthy oils vs Healthy oils

Venezuelans and Latinos still use unhealthy vegetable and corn oils for cooking, these oils are high in polyunsaturated fats which in excess can cause inflammation that can clog arteries, induce vitamin E deficiency which can lead to skin cancer. It's toxic to the liver, associated with the increase risk of cancer, heart disease and weight gain. Margarine has high content of vegetable oils and hydrogenated fats (trans fatty acids) which are highly toxic and strongly associated with heart disease. Plus, margarine is only 2 molecules away from becoming plastic.

Instead, choose organic, expeller-pressed canola oil as a healthy alternative to vegetable oil. Used in moderation, this oil is very resistant to high heat cooking. The high level of monounsaturated fatty acids found in olive oil may help lower the risk of heart disease by improving risk factors, lower cholesterol, and it may also help normalize blood clotting, benefit insulin levels and blood sugar control. Make sure to choose a high quality olive oil as many may have traces of other oils, and even diaper residual.

Look for a dark bottled, unfiltered, cold processed, extra virgin olive oil, a certified seal from any olive oil council and a harvest date to make sure is 100% pure. Olive oil is organic and therefore does not cook well in high heat as it releases toxins into the food. Organic, extra virgin coconut oil is loaded with antioxidants, can boost metabolism and help with weight loss. Coconut oil cooks very well in high heat.

Butter from grass-fed cows is heart and brain healthy, it has vitamin k2, which prevents cancer, osteoporosis and heart disease, has omega 3's, and butyrate which can fight inflammation, improve digestive health and may help prevent weight gain.

Bad sugars vs Good sugars

White refined sugar is highly toxic, it is known to suppress the immune system by reducing the amount and vitality of white blood cells. It can also affect behavior, attention and learning habits. Avoid agave and stevia as they are highly processed foods and may have harmful chemicals as the result of this.

White sugar and simple carbs cause unfriendly flora to grow in the gastrointestinal tract and disrupt estrogen metabolism. They raise blood sugar and insulin levels, resulting in adverse influences in sex hormone balance. Simple carbs have been associated with postmenopausal breast cancer. Opt for organic honey, maple syrup and raw brown sugar cane as your main sugar substitutions.

Why should you buy organic?

Many Latin spices and seasonings (sazon) contain unhealthy chemicals which should be avoided. Monosodium Glutamate (msg) is a flavor enhancer which is believed to be addictive and may cause cancer. High fructose corn syrup (hfcs) increases risks of diseases of the heart and arteries. Artificial colors like yellow #6 has been shown to cause allergic reactions like hives, rhinitis and nasal congestion. It appear to cause tumors of the kidney and adrenal glands in rats, and it may be carcinogenic. This color is banned in Norway and Sweden. Europe in general, won't accept hormone-laden U.S. beef because of the health risks.

Pesticides found in vegetables are extremely toxic which can contribute to inflammation. They are known to cause hormonal imbalance and some interfere with the body's natural hormone systems, causing an array of health problems.

Choose organic and check labels of seasonings, spices and canned foods to avoid these harmful chemicals. Opt for grass-fed, hormone-free, antibiotic-free organic beef, milk, yogurt and butter, free range eggs, chickens, broths, and fresh cheeses.

*Note: Vegetables and fruits with thick exterior skins and exteriors which are not edible, don't need to be organic.

Latest Findings on Saturated Fats

Saturated fat is heart and brain healthy. Recent research has shown that our bodies can process saturated fats easier than processed carbs and sugars. Obsessions with low-fat diets have actually increased the risk of heart disease. Experts have added that after 40 years of advising to cut saturated fat it is " the greatest medical error of our time ". They claim the guidance has left millions of people at risk of developing cardiovascular disease. Therefore it is now good to eat healthy fats like avocados, nuts, egg yolks, beef, whole milk, fatty fish, cheese and butter.

Bacon and Meats

Bacon derives from pork, it goes through a curing process with salt, nitrates and sometimes sugar among other ingredients. The fatty acids in bacon are 50% monounsaturated, 40% saturated and 10% polyunsaturated.

Bacon is as nutritious as cow meat, 100g of bacon contains 37g of high quality animal protein, vitamins b1, b2, b3, b5, b6 and b12, 89% of RDA for selenium, 53% of RDA for phosphorus, and a decent amount of iron, magnesium, zinc and potassium.

*Note: Several studies demonstrate a link between processed meat consumption, cardiovascular disease and several types of cancer. All processed meats, including bacon, should be cooked well enough to kill potential pathogens, but not burnt. There are harmful chemicals as the result of burned meats that can cause cancer.

Make sure to use a dry rub or marinade before grilling or broiling steaks and remove charred pieces after cooking all meats. For bacon and cold cuts, make sure they're organic, uncured and the animal was fed an appropriate diet. Another option is to blanch the bacon prior to use; dip in boiling water for about 3 minutes and then dip in iced water, rinse, pad dry and then cook accordingly.

Where to Shop

Local Health Food stores, Trader Joe's, Fresh Direct, Stop & Shop and Whole Foods have a wide variety of organic products. There are many local Latin food specialty stores in the U.S. and many options online are available for Venezuelan/Latin products.

Is Venezuelan food Gluten Free?

A Venezuelan research found that gluten is causing inflammation in the brain. U.S. studies have shown that gluten can cause dementia, Alzheimer's disease and depression as well. A gluten free diet is recommended for people who are allergic to wheat and other grains that contain gluten. It's also good for people who are pre-diabetics, diabetics, along with celiac disease, gluten intolerance and sensitivity which offers healthy benefits and detoxification. Most Venezuelan staples are gluten free or have very low gluten.

The Arepa Flour

Arepa is the Venezuelan traditional bread. It's made with corn/maize flour, there are many brands and variations of this flour, but " Harina P.A.N." is the first and main one. The beer and malted drink company " Empresas Polar ", developed an industrial production launching the brand in 1960. The product rapidly gained massive acceptance amongst housewives because of the tremendous saving in labor and for its high quality.

The original slogan was " se acabo la piladera " (no more pounding). It has remained unchanged since then. Pre-made arepa flour is usually made from white corn, but there are yellow corn varieties available as well. Other brands include: La Venezolana, La Colombiana, Goya Masarepa, Harina Juana, La Lucha, Donarepa, etc. If you don't live close to any Latin food store, there are many websites where you can find Harina P.A.N. among these are: amigofoods.com, amazon.com, ebay.com, and rakuten.com.

Pictures of 3 types of Harina P.A.N. From left to right: for Arepas, Empanadas and Cachapas. If you can't find all of them, you can still make empananadas and cachapas with the arepa flour (yellow bag).

*Note: The package details that is " very low gluten " and it may contain traces of wheat, oats and/or soy. If you have extreme allergies, you may want to try a gluten free, organic corn flour.

With this cookbook I intend for everyone to enjoy and learn some of the history, geography, personal stories and delicious food of a rich country with joyous people who with determination and strength will overcome any " Dark Ages " it may be going through during the publishing of this cookbook.

Here I leave you with tools to take control over your health and wish you a long nutritious life filled with great food without ever compromising on flavor. To your health, I toast!

(v) = vegetarian or vegetarian option included in the recipe
Calorie counts and cooking time are approximates

BEEF

Beef in Fresh Tomato Sauce

My dad used to make this for me when I was little, it's an easy and quick dish. He made this as a filling for arepas or you can eat it with rice too, if you'd like.

*Any kind of thinly sliced beef will work well with this recipe.

Cooking time: 25 minutes

½ lb grass-fed chuck, bottom round or eye round beef, thinly sliced
½ teaspoon ground cumin
iodized sea salt
2 tablespoons extra virgin olive oil
1 onion, sliced crosswise
2 organic tomatoes, chopped
½ cup filtered water

Rub beef with salt and cumin and set aside. Let stand for 15 minutes. In a medium pan, heat oil over medium high heat, add the onion and saute until soft, about 5 minutes.

Add the beef and cook for 10 minutes, or until brown. Pour the tomatoes and the water. Simmer until sauce is blended, around 10 minutes.

Serves 1 ½ cups
½ cup = 310 calories

Churrasco (choo. rras. Coh)
Grilled Steak

This is a favorite in steak restaurants all over Venezuela. It's simple and quick to make at home too.

Cooking time: 8-10 minutes

1 lb grass - fed sirloin steak

For marinade:
$\frac{1}{2}$ teaspoon garlic paste
$\frac{1}{2}$ teaspoon ground cumin
$\frac{1}{2}$ teaspoon oregano
1 tablespoon organic Worcestershire sauce
1 tablespoon lime juice
iodized sea salt
pepper

Marinade the steak and let it stand for 30 minutes at room temperature.

Grill in grilling pan on high for 4 minutes on each side for a medium to medium-rare steak, depending on thickness.

Serves 1-2 portions
$\frac{1}{4}$ lb = 250 calories

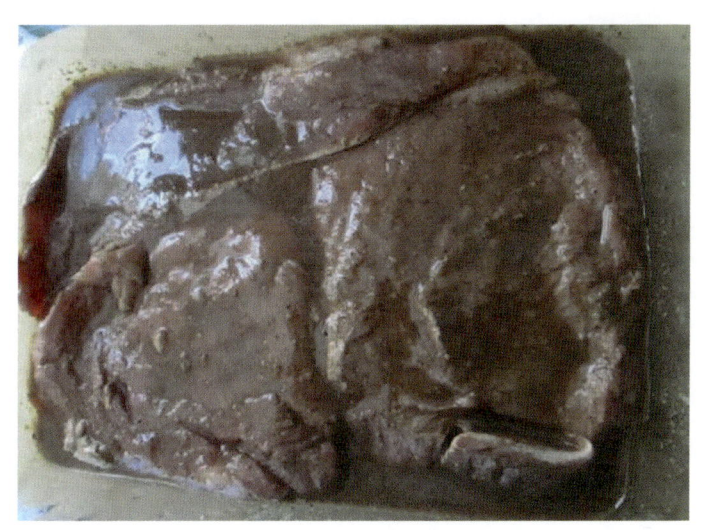

Coconut Goat Stew

This creamy, mild dish is commonly found in the occidental region of Venezuela, mostly in Zulia state.

Cooking time: 1h and 40 minutes

1 lb organic goat meat with bones, cleaned and cut into squares
4 cups filtered water
2 tablespoons annatto infused organic virgin coconut oil (pg 146)
1 onion, chopped
2 garlic cloves, minced or 1 teaspoon garlic paste
1 organic green pepper, seeded and chopped
2 organic tomatoes, chopped
1 can organic light coconut milk
1 teaspoon cumin powder
iodized sea salt
1 tablespoon fresh lime juice

Boil the goat in 4 cups of water in a medium pot over high heat until soft, about 1 hour.

In a separate sauce pan, make the " sofrito " (pg 118) by sauteing the onion, garlic, green pepper and tomatoes in the annatto infused coconut oil until soft, about 5-10 minutes.

Add the sofrito mixture, coconut milk, cumin and salt to the goat. Simmer over medium heat until all ingredients are blended and sauce thickens, about 20-30 minutes. Sprinkle with lime juice and serve with white rice, tostones and/or salad.

Makes 3 cups
1 cup = 400 calories

Goat Tarkari (tar. kah. Ree)

The history of this dish starts once upon a time in the Caribbean island of Trinidad, handed over to the British in 1802 and transformed into the center of diffusion of Indian culture with the arrival of Hindus after the abolition of slavery in 1839 and extended all over the Caribbean and parts of Venezuela.

Preparation and cooking time: 1 h and 40 minutes

1 lb organic goat meat with bones, cleaned and cut into pieces
For marinade:
1 fresh lime juice
1 teaspoon curry powder
1 teaspoon cumin powder
iodized sea salt
For stew:
2 tablespoons extra virgin olive oil
1 teaspoon curry powder
1 teaspoon cumin powder
1 onion, chopped
1 teaspoon garlic-ginger paste*
2 organic sweet peppers, chopped
2 organic tomatoes, chopped
4-6 cups filtered water
1 tablespoon organic cilantro, chopped

Marinade the goat in the lime juice, curry, cumin and salt. Let stand for 20 minutes. In a medium pot, heat olive oil over medium heat and add curry and cumin powder. Stir and cook for 2 minutes. Add the onion, garlic-ginger paste and sweet peppers. Simmer for 5-10 minutes, until soft.
Add the goat and cook until lightly brown, about 5-10 minutes. Pour the tomatoes and water, cover and cook over medium-high heat for 1 hour or until goat meat is soft. Sprinkle with cilantro and serve with rice and tostones.

Makes 4 cups
1 cup = 430 calories

*Found in Indian grocery stores

Ground Beef & Tomatoes

This recipe is a Latin version of the Italian Bolognese sauce. It is used as a filling for arepas, empanadas and as a main course with rice. The empanada filling should be on the dry side to avoid the empanada from braking apart while being cooked.

Cooking time: 30 minutes

1 tablespoon extra virgin olive oil
1 onion, chopped
2 garlic cloves, minced
½ lb grass fed ground beef
1 tablespoon organic Worcestershire sauce
1 teaspoon ground cumin
iodized sea salt
1 teaspoon oregano
1 organic tomato, chopped
¼ cup organic beef broth
pinch of tabasco sauce

Rinse the ground beef with water in a colander before cooking. Beef will lose some of its color, turning pinkish. Heat olive oil over medium heat, add the onion and garlic and cook until soft, about 5 minutes.

Lightly brown the ground beef with the onion for 10 min. Add Worcestershire sauce, cumin, salt and oregano. Stir to combine and add the tomato, beef broth and tabasco. Stir and simmer on medium-high heat until sauce thickens, about 15 more minutes.

Serves 2 cups
1 cup ground beef = 300 calories

*Ground beef can be a substitute for shredded beef in a pabellon

Parrilla (pa. Ree. Yah)

Parrilla is basically steaks cooked on an outdoor charcoal grill, often adding chorizo, blood sausage and tripe to the grill and making " parrilla mixta ". But if you live in an apartment in NYC, like me, just use a grilling pan.

My uncle used to make this on weekends for either someone's birthday, holidays or as an excuse for a get together with the family. Usually accompanied with boiled yuca, salad, guasacaca sauce and maybe a sancocho soup too.

I remember sitting outdoors by the pool in one of my family reunions, listening to loud music and laughing at people arguing playfully over a long game of dominos. Starving while waiting for the parrilla to be ready, it just took them forever to get the charcoal grill started!

Cooking time: 8-10 minutes

2-3 lbs grass-fed sirloin, top round, or strip loins
10 garlic cloves, minced or 5 teaspoons garlic paste
iodized sea salt
pepper
2-3 bottles (gluten free)beer (pilsner, pale lager, blond ale or pale ale)

Rub beef with the garlic, salt, pepper and marinade in beer for 1-2 hours at room temperature.

Prepare charcoal grill and cook steak whole. If you're using a grilling pan, make sure the grill is very hot before adding the steak.

Cook on high for 4 minutes on each side for a medium to medium-rare steak, depending on thickness.

Serves 8-10 people
1 medium steak = 290 calories

*Cooking beef marinated in beer reduces the risk of cancer up to 53%

Shredded Beef (v)

This special type of beef served in a Pabellon (pa_. be_' ʎo_n)pg 182, which is the Venezuelan typical platter, is served with white rice, black beans and sweet plantains or tostones. In the flatlands and the country they add a fried egg on top. In arepa joints in Venezuela they serve 2 kinds of shredded beef for arepa fillings, the dry one and the regular one with fresh tomato sauce. I will give you both versions.

Cooking time: for dry-25 minutes
for reg-40 minutes

1 lb grass-fed skirt steak, cut into pieces (substitute with peeled eggplant, cut into strips for vegetarian)*
filtered water
1 onion, cut in half
3 garlic cloves, cut in halves
1 organic green or red bell pepper, cut into pieces
1 bay leaf
iodized sea salt

For the dry shredded beef:
2 tablespoons extra virgin olive oil
1 onion, sliced crosswise
1 tablespoon lemon juice

For the regular shredded beef add:
2 organic tomatoes, chopped
2 cups organic beef broth made from the previous boil
1 tablespoon organic Worcestershire sauce

Boil the skirt steak or eggplant in enough water to cover over medium high heat with the halved onion, garlic, bell pepper, bay leaf and salt for 10 min. Remove from heat and reserve the broth for later if making the regular type shredded beef. Take the steak out of the water, let stand and shred with a fork or by hand when it's cool enough to handle.

For the dry shredded beef:
Heat olive oil in a medium sauce pan over medium heat, add the sliced onion and the shredded beef at the same time. Cook until both onion

and beef are browned, caramelized and crispy, about 10-15 minutes. Add salt to taste and lemon juice to bring out the flavor.

For the regular shredded beef:
 Heat olive oil in a medium sauce pan over medium heat. Cook the onion in the olive oil (chop the onion instead if desired) and saute until soft, about 5 minutes. Add the beef, tomatoes, Worcestershire sauce and beef broth. Simmer on medium high heat until sauce is smooth, about 20-30 minutes.

Serves 1 cup dry and 1 ½ cups regular
½ cup = 200 calories

* For vegetarian just use eggplant and follow the recipe as is

The Nomad's Skirt Steak

This is one of my favorite dishes and my own invention. I tend to like strong flavors and this thin, fatty steak makes marinades sink deeply in between its grains and the result is a juicy, melt-in-your-mouth, spicy goodness.

Cooking time: 10 minutes

1 lb grass-fed skirt steak
½ teaspoon lemon-pepper powder
½ teaspoon cumin powder
½ teaspoon paprika
1 teaspoon garlic paste
1 tablespoon lemon juice
1 tablespoon extra virgin olive oil
iodized sea salt
pinch pepper
1 teaspoon organic dried parsley or oregano

Marinade steak with all the ingredients and let the flavors sink in anywhere from 30 minutes to 1 hour.

Broil for 5 minutes on each side for a medium-well steak.

Serves 3-4 portions
¼ lb = 232 calories

CHICKEN

Chicken and Potato Stew

Cooking time: 45 minutes

1 tablespoons extra virgin olive oil
1 tablespoon organic butter
1 onion, cut crosswise
1 ½ lb organic free range boneless, skinless chicken thighs, cut in pieces
3 organic tomatoes, cut into 4 pieces each
3 garlic cloves
1 organic green bell pepper, cut into 4 pieces
½ cup dry white wine
1 cup filtered water
½ teaspoon ground cumin
½ teaspoon oregano
1 teaspoon iodized sea salt
1 tablespoon lime juice
1-2 organic potatoes, peeled and sliced
½ tablespoon capers, rinsed and chopped
1 cup fresh or frozen peas
1 tablespoon organic parsley, chopped

In a medium pot, saute the onion in the olive oil and butter over medium heat until soft, about 5 minutes. Add the chicken and cook until golden brown, about 10 minutes.

Blend the tomatoes, garlic, green pepper, white wine, water, cumin, oregano, salt and lime juice, and add to the chicken. Add the potatoes and the capers, simmer over medium high heat for 15 minutes.

Add the peas, stir, cover and cook over medium low heat for another 10-15 minutes or until sauce is thick. Remove from heat and sprinkle with parsley. Let stand for 5 minutes before serving.

Serves 4 portions
1 cup = 310 calories

Chicken Croquettes

This dish is the result of our French-Mediterranean cuisine heritage. You can find this in many restaurants in Venezuela as an appetizer and at food courts in malls as a snack, often served with a German or tartar sauce.

Cooking time: 35 minutes

2 chicken breasts, skinned and cooked
3 tablespoons organic butter
1 tablespoon organic canola oil
1 large onion, chopped
1 teaspoon garlic paste
1 organic red pepper, chopped
½ teaspoon turmeric
½ teaspoon ground oregano
½ teaspoon garlic powder
iodized sea salt
pepper
5 tablespoons corn flour (P.A.N.) or gluten free flour
1 cup organic, free range, low sodium chicken broth
1 cup organic whole milk
1 tablespoon organic parsley, chopped
organic whole grain gluten free bread crumbs
garlic powder
paprika
dried parsley or oregano
2 organic free range eggs
extra virgin olive oil

Shred or cut chicken breasts into very small pieces, set aside. Heat butter and canola oil in a sauce pan over medium heat, add the onion, garlic and red bell pepper. Cook until soft, about 5 minutes. Add turmeric, oregano, garlic powder, sea salt and pepper, stir. Then, add flour, tablespoon by tablespoon and stirring constantly. Add broth and milk slowly, stirring constantly. Cook for about 10 minutes. Remove from heat. Add the shredded chicken and parsley, mix to form a paste and refrigerate for 3 hours.

Pre-heat oven at 400F. Spread bread crumbs on a plate, sprinkle with garlic powder, paprika and dried parsley or oregano and mix well. Lightly beat the eggs in a medium bowl. Rub olive oil on a baking sheet with a paper towel or brush.

Make small balls with chicken paste, dip in eggs, and roll over bread crumbs to cover. Place on baking sheet and bake for 20 minutes until golden brown.

Makes 13-14 medium sized croquettes.
1 medium croquette = 120 calories

Chicken Provenzal

With Mediterranean roots, the results of this dish is a tender juicy chicken with soft textures and deep flavors. I prefer to blend the sauce ingredients and save time.

Cooking time: 40 minutes

½ organic free range chicken, cut into pieces
iodized sea salt
pepper
1 tablespoon reg flour or gluten-free flour
2 tablespoons extra virgin olive oil
1 onion, cut into 4 pieces
1 green bell pepper, seeded and cut into 4 pieces
2 cloves garlic, minced or 1 teaspoon garlic paste
2-3 tomatoes, cut into 4 pieces each
1 cup red wine
1 cup organic, free range, low-sodium chicken broth
½ teaspoon oregano
1 bay leaf

Rinse chicken and pat dry with a paper towel. Rub the chicken lightly with the salt and pepper. Coat with the flour and set aside. Blend all the ingredients except for the bay leaf and oregano, set aside.

In a medium pot, saute the chicken pieces in the olive oil over medium heat until light brown, about 3-5 minutes on each side. Pour blended mixture, bay leaf and oregano.

Simmer over medium heat until the chicken is cooked through and sauce thickens, about 30 minutes. Let stand for 5 minutes before serving.

Serves 3-4 cups.
1 cup = 290 calories

Shredded Chicken (v)

The intensity and warmth of this comforting chicken is mild, soothing and will give you a taste of Venezuelan vibe in your palate. This chicken is easy and simple to make. The chicken can be boiled, baked or grilled before adding it to the sofrito which keeps the chicken moist and hearty.

* Substitute chicken breast with peeled zucchini for a vegetarian option. Cut into strips and skip the baking.

Cooking time: 40 minutes

1 organic free range chicken breast
2 tablespoons extra virgin olive oil
1 onion, sliced crosswise
2 organic tomatoes, chopped
1 cup organic, free range, low sodium chicken broth (use organic vegetable broth for vegetarian)
iodized sea salt

Pre-heat oven at 400 F. Bake chicken breast for 15 minutes. Remove from oven and let cool a bit. Shred the chicken with a fork or by hand. Saute the onion in the olive oil until soft, about 5 minutes and add the chicken (zucchini).

Cook until chicken is lightly brown and caramelized. Add the tomatoes and the broth. Sprinkle with salt and simmer over medium heat until blended through, about 20 minutes (10 minutes for the zucchini).

This can be used as a filling for arepas, empanadas (make sure it's dry), served with white rice and even tostones (see picture).

Makes 2 cups
½ cup = 105 calories

*For grilled chicken, grill breast for 5 minutes on each side before adding it to the sofrito.

DRINKS

Three in One Juice

This antioxidant, anti-inflammatory and detox packed juice is great for hangover days. It has vitamin a, vitamin c, calcium, potassium and it's cancer, heart disease and stroke preventive.

Research show that drinking 1 glass of beet juice a day, decreases high blood pressure for up to 30%.

Preparation time: 20 minutes

1 organic beet bunch, peeled
4 cups fresh orange juice
1 cup organic baby carrots
4 tablespoons organic honey

Cut beets and baby carrots into pieces and blend on high with the orange juice.

Place juice through a colander into a jug (unless you prefer to chew your juice), and add the honey.

Makes 3 cups.
1 glass (8 oz) = 74 calories

Aloe Vera juice

This is a detox juice and is best taken in the mornings on an empty stomach.

Preparation time: 15 minutes

1 aloe vera leaf
1 cup pineapple
½ cucumber
1 cup raw coconut water
1 tablespoon organic honey

Peel and cut the aloe vera. Place in a blender with peeled pineapple cut into pieces, discarding hard middle.

Add cucumber, cut into pieces, and coconut water.
Run blender on medium for 2-3 minutes.

Press through a colander into an iced glass. Add honey and stir.

Serve 2 ¼ cups
1 glass = 200 calories

Papaya Juice

Papaya is originally from Central America. It contains vitamins a, c, and b complex, potassium, magnesium, fiber, folic acid, small amounts of iron, calcium and folate, which is a type of vitamin b required for the production of red blood cells, besides being a great digestive assistant.

Healing properties: antioxidant, kidneys, liver and ovaries anti-inflammatory, prevents breast and colon cancer, rejuvenates, protects the heart, prevents gastritis and bloating. Alleviates the symptoms of gastroenteritis, colitis and irritated colon.

Prevents and assists gastric ulcers. It's low in calories and high in fiber and nutrients which can be used in weight loss diets.

Preparation time: 15 minutes

½ medium papaya
2 cups filtered water
2 tablespoons organic honey
¼ teaspoon pure vanilla extract
pinch nutmeg
pinch cinnamon
¼ cup organic whole milk (optional)

Peel, seed and cut papaya in small pieces and add to a blender with water. Add honey, vanilla, nutmeg and cinnamon and blend until smooth. Pour in a glass, add milk if desired. Stir and add ice cubes.

Serves about 3 ½ glasses
1 glass = 70 calories (adding ¼ cup milk = 107 calories)

Papelon con limon (pah. peh. Lon. con. lee. Mon) Sugar Cane Loaf with Lime

This Venezuelan version of a lemonade is not only refreshing, is healthier than the refined sugary one." Papelon " is a hardened unrefined sugarcane. Sold mostly at Latin or Spanish markets as panela.

Papelon is considered a food and unlike sugar, which is sucrose, it shows significant contents of glucose, fructose, protein, minerals (such as calcium, iron, copper and phosphorus) and vitamins, such as ascorbic acid and b complex.

It's been attributed many beneficial effects in the treatment of colds, taking it as a hot drink with lime, which hydrates and reduces discomfort. The cold papelon version is commonly used by athletes as a natural sports drink that not only refreshes, but provides calories and minerals for optimum performance and endurance. Researchers have detected hydrating and healing properties in the treatment of varicose ulcers and sinusitis.

Preparation time: 30 minutes

1/3 cup papelon
1 lime juice
3 cups warm filtered water

Shave the papelon with a knife. Heat the water in a small pot over medium heat, do not boil. Soften the shaved papelon by letting it stand in the warm water for 20 minutes.

Add the lime juice and stir. Refrigerate 1 hour before serving and pour over ice cubes.

Serves 3 glasses.
1 glass = 150 calories

Pineapple Cocada (co.ca.tha.)

This is a combination of a traditional Venezuelan cocada and a virgin pina colada.

Preparation time: 15 minutes

2 cups coconut milk
1 cup pineapple
2 teaspoons maple syrup
splash pure vanilla extract
cinnamon powder

Rinse and cut the pineapple crosswise, peel and cut into cubes. Discard hard center.

Blend the coconut milk and pineapple with the honey and vanilla extract.

Pour over ice cubes with a sprinkle of cinnamon powder on top.

Serves 2 glasses
1 glass = 220 calories

Pumpkin Juice

Pumpkins are loaded with the antioxidant, beta-carotene (vitamin a), which reduces the risk of developing certain types of cancer and offers protection against heart disease.

Preparation time: 25 minutes

½ lb pumpkin, chopped, peeled and seeded
4 cups filtered water
2 cinnamon sticks
3 tablespoons organic honey or maple syrup
½ teaspoon nutmeg
organic whole milk (optional)

Cover the pumpkin with water and boil with the cinnamon sticks until a fork cuts easily through the pumpkin, about 15-20 minutes. Let it cool at room temperature, discard cinnamon sticks.

Blend pumpkin with its water, honey and nutmeg on high until smooth. Add a bit of milk, if desired, the same day you will drink the juice, otherwise it will go bad. Refrigerate leftovers.

Serves 4 cups
1 glass = 130 calories

Sesame Seed Juice

There are many places in Venezuela where they only specialize in serving natural juices. They also serve them together with arepas in " fast food " joints.

Sesame seeds are rich in vitamin b and e, fiber, good fat, minerals, antioxidants and protein.

Preparation time: 10 minutes

1 cup sesame seeds
4 cups filtered water
1 teaspoon maple syrup
pinch cinnamon

Dry roast the sesame seeds in a small pan over low heat. Stirring constantly until they start to turn golden brown.

Do not let them get too dark or they will taste bitter. Remove from heat and let stand for 5 minutes.

Blend the roasted sesame seeds in the water. Drain the juice through a colander, add the honey and serve.

You can use organic milk instead of water for a " batido " (smoothie) type drink instead. Pour over a glass filled with ice cubes and sprinkle with cinnamon.

Serves 4 glasses.
1 glass = 280 calories

Tizana (tee. Sah. Nah)

This drink is very similar to a sangria, but without the alcohol. In Venezuela when I was little, my grandfather had a " bodega " in the garage of his house and he used to serve homemade tizana. It was refreshing, but made from kool-aid. Here's a better version…

Preparation time: 10 minutes

2 cups organic cranberry or pomegranate juice from concentrate
2 cups raw coconut water
2 cups cut up fruits such as: pineapple, papaya, cantaloupe, organic grapes, etc.
1 tablespoon star anise
4 teaspoons organic honey

Mix cranberry or pomegranate juice with coconut water. Add the cut up fruits, star anise and honey.

Stir and refrigerate for 30 minutes before serving.

Makes 4-5 glasses
1 glass = 140 calories

Watermelon and Pineapple Juice

Watermelons contain 6% sugar and 91% water. They're a big source of vitamin c, contains large amounts of carotenoids and a significant source of lycopene. It's a mild diuretic and research indicates they may have anti-hypertensive effects.

Pineapple is an excellent source of manganese and vitamin c. It's used in many cases to fight toxins in the body. Great combination for a refreshing and healthy drink.

Preparation time: 15 minutes

1 cup watermelon, peeled and seeded
1 cup pineapple
1 tablespoons organic honey
1 cup organic raw coconut water

Rinse pineapple and slice crosswise with a big knife. Peel each slice, cut into small pieces and discard the hard middle. Cut the watermelon in small pieces.

Blend watermelon, pineapple in the coconut water on high. Press pulp through sieve into jug, discard pulp. Add honey and stir with a wooden spoon. Keep refrigerated.

Makes 2 cups
1 glass = 92 calories

FISH AND SEAFOOD

Baked Snapper

Red snapper is a very common fish cooked in Venezuela. It's always served whole with rice and vegetables or salad.

Cooking time: 20 minutes

1 wild caught, whole red snapper
1 tablespoon extra-virgin olive oil
1 cup seafood or vegetable broth
1 lime juice
1 teaspoon organic Worcestershire sauce
iodized sea salt
pepper

Pre-heat oven at 400 F.

Rinse and clean fish taking off all scales with the back of a knife. Make an incision in the bottom of the fish to separate the fillets.

Sprinkle with salt and pepper on the inside of the fish. Lay the fish in the baking dish.

Mix the olive oil, fish broth, lime juice and Worcestershire sauce and pour on top of the fish making sure some of the sauce goes under the fish as well. Bake for 20 minutes.

Serves 2-3 portions
1 fillet = 210 calories

Broiled Mahi-mahi in Adobo Rub

Asian adobo and Latin adobo have different flavors. The Latin one is a dry rub consisting of mainly powdered garlic, turmeric, oregano, salt and pepper. It can be used for fish, chicken and beef as well.

This is a very simple and quick recipe.

Cooking time: 5 minutes

2 mahi-mahi or tilapia fillets
½ teaspoon garlic paste
½ teaspoon turmeric
½ teaspoon oregano
pinch iodized sea salt
pinch pepper
fresh lime juice
extra-virgin olive oil

Rinse fish and pat dry with a paper towel. Rub olive oil, garlic paste, turmeric, oregano, salt and pepper on both sides of the fillets.

Place on a baking sheet previously rubbed with olive oil. Broil for 5 minutes. Sprinkle lime juice over the fish and serve.

Makes 2 portions
1 fillet = 270 calories

*Fish is better cooked medium-rare for the best absorption of its nutritious properties

Calamari Stew

This calamari stew is a light, warm, quick and easy recipe with Mediterranean roots. Serve with rice, tostones or veggies.

Cooking time: 30 minutes

1-2 tablespoon of extra virgin olive oil
1 onion, cut crosswise
1 organic red pepper, cut into thin strips
½ teaspoon minced garlic or garlic paste
2 tablespoons organic scallions, chopped
3 organic tomatoes, chopped
½ lb calamari, cleaned and thinly sliced
2 teaspoons organic fresh parsley, finely chopped

Saute the onion, red pepper, garlic and scallion in the olive oil until soft, about 5 minutes. Add the tomatoes, cook for 10 minutes.

Add calamari and simmer over medium heat for 15 more minutes. Remove from heat. Sprinkle with the parsley before serving.

Serves 3 portions
1 cup = 200 calories

Pan-Fried Whole Grouper

This is the typical fried whole fish you get at the beach in Venezuela. Right out of the ocean fresh. Usually served with tostones and avocado salad. You may substitute with any other firm textured fish.

Cooking time: 6 minutes

1 wild caught, whole grouper (substitute with cod, striped or sea bass, mahi-mahi, catfish, or red snapper)
4 tablespoons organic extra virgin coconut oil
iodized sea salt
freshly squeezed lime juice

Clean and rinse fish, making sure to take off all the scales with the back of a knife. Pad dry with a paper towel.

Heat the coconut oil on high heat, add the fish when the oil is very hot. Pan-fry for 3 minutes on each side.

Remove from heat, squeeze lime juice and add salt.

Serves 2-3 portions
1 fillet = 230 calories

Rompe Colchon
(Roam. peh. coal. Choan) Matress Braker

There's always someone selling this in plastic containers at the beaches in Venezuela. It has many names: " back to life, 7 potencies, awaken the dead, etc ". It's used as a remedy for hangovers and is also considered an aphrodisiac cocktail. It's basically a seafood marinade made to be eaten at room temperature or cold.

Cooking time: 20 minutes

filtered water
¼ lb calamari, cleaned and sliced
¼ lb octopus, cleaned
¼ lb mussels, cleaned
¼ lb clams, cleaned
¼ lb oysters, cleaned
¼ lb shrimp, peeled and deveined
1 onion, finely chopped
½ organic green pepper, finely chopped
1 fresh orange juice
1 fresh lime juice
¼ cup white wine vinegar
¼ cup filtered water
1 tablespoon organic Worcestershire sauce
½ tablespoon organic ketchup or tomato paste
iodized sea salt
pepper
1 teaspoon tabasco sauce (optional)

Boil enough water to cover seafood, add salt, calamari, octopus, mussels, clams and oysters, cook for 15 minutes, add shrimp and remove from heat. Let it stand for 5 minutes. Remove seafood from hot water and add to a large bowl with cold water. Let it stand for 10 minutes, remove from water. Take all the shells off mussels, clams and oysters.

In a large bowl combine the onion, green pepper, orange juice, lime juice, white wine vinegar, water, Worcestershire sauce, ketchup, salt, pepper and tabasco. Mix well and add the seafood to the marinade. Refrigerate in an air-tight container for 24 hours before serving.

Serves 4
1 cup = 315 calories

*Rompe Colchon can be served by itself or with crackers

Seafood Casserole

My uncle loves to cook seafood and every time we visited him, he would be making a seafood or shrimp casserole. I've stolen his recipe and add it to this cookbook. Don't worry, he'll never find out.

Cooking time: 30 minutes

½ lb octopus
½ lb calamari
½ lb shrimp, peeled and deveined
2 tablespoon extra-virgin olive oil
1 onion
3 cloves garlic
1 organic red bell pepper
4 organic tomatoes
1 bay leaf
1 tablespoon organic tomato paste
iodized sea salt
pepper
½ cup filtered water
1 tablespoon organic fresh parsley

Chop or blend the onion, garlic, red bell pepper and tomato, set aside. Saute the octopus in the olive oil over medium heat for 15 minutes and add the blended onion mix.

Add bay leaf, tomato paste, salt, pepper and water. Stir and add the calamari. Simmer and reduce sauce for 10 minutes. Remove from heat and add shrimp and parsley. Let stand for 5 minutes.

Serves 3 cups
1 cup = 170 calories

Venezuelan style Bacalao
(bah. kah. La. Oh)

I remember, growing up catholic in Venezuela, we couldn't eat meat during holy week. We always ate "chiguire" (cheeh. Wee. Rae) instead. It tasted just like fish and it looked just like fish at the store, so I never questioned it.

As a teenager, I found out that chiguire was not a fish, but a dog-like, hairy rodent. I had never seen one in person, but pictures were enough. I didn't know if I should've felt disgusted or sorry. And again, just like I had been lied to about Santa, I had been lied to about what I was eating. Anyway, I had already eaten it and it tasted good, so why stop? Here's a simple recipe for a real bacalao.

Cooking time: 25 minutes

1 lb bacalao fillets (substitute with cod or pollock fillets)
2 tablespoons extra-virgin olive oil
1 onion, finely chopped
3 organic tomatoes, chopped
½ cup filtered water

Soak bacalao in water from one day to another, discard water and rinse. Add to boiling water and cook for 10 minutes. Let cool. Discard water and rinse again, making sure all the salt is washed away. Brake fish into small pieces with a fork or by hand.

Saute onion until soft, about 5 minutes, add fish and cook over medium heat for 5 minutes. Add the tomatoes and ½ cup water. Cook until the fish is blended with the tomato, about 10-15 minutes.

Makes 2-3 cups
1 cup = 200 calories

RICE

Arroz con pollo
(a. RRos. con. Poh. yoh.) Rice with chicken

Arroz con pollo is a traditional South American dish. The recipe differs from country to country and it's originally from Spain. It's usually served at parties and special occasions.

Preparation and cooking time: 45 minutes

1 organic free range chicken, skinned and cut into small pieces
1 teaspoon garlic powder
1 teaspoon turmeric powder
1 teaspoon oregano powder
1 teaspoon cumin powder
iodized sea salt
pepper
2 tablespoons extra virgin olive oil
1 tablespoon organic butter
1 onion, chopped
2 cloves garlic, minced
2 organic carrots, finely chopped
1 tablespoon capers, chopped
1 cup stuffed green olives, sliced in half
3 teaspoons mustard
3 tablespoon organic Worcestershire sauce
4 cups basmati rice
8 cups free range low-sodium chicken broth
1 cup fresh or frozen peas
1 cup fresh or frozen whole kernel corn

Rub the chicken with the garlic powder, turmeric, oregano, cumin, sea salt and pepper, set aside. In a large deep pot, saute the onion, garlic and carrots in the olive oil and butter over medium heat until soft, about 5 minutes.

Add the seasoned chicken to the onion mixture. Cook until chicken is slightly brown, about 5 minutes on each side. Add the capers, green olives, mustard and Worcestershire sauce. Add the rice and stir for 2 minutes.

Add the broth and simmer on medium high heat until half the broth has evaporated, add the peas and corn. Cook on medium low until rice is cooked through, 20-30 minutes. Adjust salt if needed and serve.

Serves 8-10 people
1 cup = 325 calories

Rice & Shrimp

This recipe is very similar to a Spanish " Paella ", but with a few differences.

Cooking time: 32 minutes

2 tablespoons extra virgin olive oil
1 onion, chopped
2 cloves garlic, minced
1 organic red or green pepper, chopped
1 organic tomato, chopped
1 cup basmati rice
½ cup white wine
3 cups seafood broth
½ teaspoon ground oregano
1 bay leaf
iodized sea salt
pepper
½ teaspoon annatto powder
1 tablespoon organic Worcestershire sauce
½ lb shrimp, peeled and deveined
1 tablespoon organic cilantro or parsley

Saute the onion, garlic, pepper and tomato in the olive oil over medium heat until soft, about 5 minutes. Add the rice, stir and cook for 2 minutes. Pour the white wine, broth, oregano, bay leaf, sea salt and pepper.

Stir and add the annatto powder and Worcestershire sauce. Simmer uncovered, stirring occasionally until rice is almost ready, between 10 and 15 minutes. Add the shrimp and cilantro.

Stir, cover and turn off the heat. Leave the rice and shrimp cook with its own steam for about 5 minutes, discard bay leaf.

Serves 3 cups
1 cup = 235 calories

Seafood Soupy Rice

I don't make "Asopao" as often as I should and I'm very much inclined to savior anything soupy and saucy. You can make chicken soupy rice instead or add crispy organic bacon to the seafood one. This is a simple recipe inspired by the Caribbean flavors of Margarita, a Venezuelan island located on the east coast, close to Trinidad and Tobago.

Preparation and cooking time: 50 minutes

2 tablespoons extra virgin olive oil
1 onion, chopped
2 garlic cloves, minced
1 organic red pepper, chopped
1 organic green pepper, chopped
1 tablespoon organic parsley
1 tablespoon organic cilantro
2 tablespoon organic tomato paste
½ teaspoon ground cumin
½ teaspoon ground oregano
iodized sea salt
pepper
¼ lb octopus, cleaned and cut
¼ lb calamari, cleaned and sliced
4 clams, in their shell, cleaned
12 mussels, in their shell, cleaned
¼ cup sherry wine
1 cup basmati rice
6-7 cups seafood broth
pinch of turmeric for coloring
½ lb shrimp, peeled and deveined
lime juice

In a large pot, saute the onion, garlic, peppers, herbs, tomato paste and spices in the olive oil for 5 minutes over medium heat. Add the octopus, calamari, clams and mussels. Stir and add the sherry wine.

Add the rice, stir and cook for 2 minutes. Add broth and pinch of turmeric, stir. Cook for 10 minutes, add shrimp and remove from heat. Let stand for 5 minutes, making sure it still maintains the consistency of a soup. Sprinkle lime juice right before eating.

Serves 8 cups
1 cup = 300 calories

White rice

My mom has never liked to eat chunks of onions, whether cooked or raw, but she does like its flavor. This is how I learned to make white rice from her, by adding a whole small onion to the water to give it an onion taste without having to actually see and eat onion chunks. I prefer rice to be creamy so I tend to add a little more water than most people.

Cooking time: 20 minutes

1 small onion, peeled
2 ¾ cup filtered water
1 tablespoon extra-virgin coconut or olive oil
½ teaspoon iodized sea salt
1 cup white rice (basmati and sushi rice have lower glycemic index content than regular rice, therefore, they won't raise your blood sugar levels)
organic red pepper, cut into fine strips (optional)
organic whole cilantro stalks (optional)

Cook onion in the water on high heat in a pot. When it starts boiling, about 5 minutes, add the olive oil, the salt and the rice. Stir and cover for 5 minutes.

Once the water starts boiling again, uncover and stir. Lower the heat to medium and cook for another 5 minutes. Stir and turn heat to low.

You can add the red pepper at this point, cook until water is completely vaporized and rice is creamy and firm, about 5 minutes longer.

Sprinkle whole cilantro on top to add aroma, cover and let stand for 5 minutes. Discard onion and cilantro.

Serves 3 cups
½ cup = 100 calories

SALADS

Avocado and Shrimp Salad (v)

Preparation time: 15 minutes

6 leaves organic romaine lettuce
1 organic tomato, chopped
½ cup (8 oz) fresh black olives (Do Not buy canned black olives, they have no nutritional value nor flavor)
¼ hass avocado, peeled and chopped
¼ lb shrimp, peeled and deveined (discard for vegetarian)
1 tablespoon extra-virgin olive oil
1 tablespoon fresh lime juice
iodized sea salt
pepper
2 tablespoons white cheese or feta, chopped (optional)

Rinse lettuce and tomato. Chop lettuce, tomatoes and avocado. Boil enough water in a pot, add the shrimp and cook for 5 minutes, drain and let cool.

Add shrimp and black olives to the salad together with the olive oil, lime juice, salt and pepper.

Serves 4 cups
1 cup = 65 calories

Beet and Potato Salad (v)

This is my mom's recipe, she used to make this for lunch on hot summer weekends in Venezuela.

Preparation and cooking time: 1 hour

4 organic romaine lettuce leaves
organic water crest bunch
1 medium organic beet
1 medium organic potato
1 large organic tomato, sliced crosswise
Dressing:
1 tablespoon extra-virgin olive oil
2 tablespoons balsamic vinegar
iodized sea salt

Preheat oven at 400F.

Roast beet and potato on a baking sheet for 45 minutes. Rinse lettuce and water crest. Dry separately in salad spinner.

Place lettuce leaves on a platter, and the sliced tomato on top. Peel and slice potato and beet, place on top of the tomato.

Place water crest in the center of the salad. Drizzle with the olive oil and balsamic vinegar. Sprinkle with sea salt.

Serves 4 portions
1 cup = 110 calories

Cabbage Salad (v)

This salad is commonly served over tostones at the beach and on hot dogs, pepitos and hamburgers at fast food joints. The dressing is usually made with mayo, but here's a yogurt based version.

Preparation time: 20 minutes

$\frac{1}{4}$ cabbage
2 organic carrots
1 tablespoon organic cilantro

yogurt dressing: (optional)
$\frac{1}{2}$ cup organic plain yogurt
$\frac{1}{2}$ teaspoon onion powder
1 teaspoon mustard
1 tablespoon lemon juice
1 tablespoon Worcestershire sauce
1 tablespoon extra-virgin olive oil
pinch of tabasco sauce
$\frac{1}{2}$ teaspoon iodized sea salt
$\frac{1}{2}$ teaspoon honey

Shred the cabbage, peel and shred the carrots and finely chop the cilantro, mix in a medium bowl.

Make yogurt dressing in a separate small bowl and mix with cabbage salad.

Serves 2 cups
1 cup = 160 calories

The Nomad Cook's Criolla Salad
(v)

Well, this is one of my inventions. It's quick and easy to make. You can pretty much add or subtract anything in this salad.

Preparation time: 20 minutes

$\frac{1}{2}$ organic romaine lettuce, chopped
2 organic tomatoes, chopped
$\frac{1}{2}$ lb cooked, organic, ham or turkey breast, chopped (discard for vegetarian)
$\frac{1}{4}$ lb fresh feta cheese, chopped (optional)
1 avocado, peeled and chopped
$\frac{1}{2}$ can or jar (8oz) palm tree
$\frac{1}{2}$ small can, low sodium whole kernel corn
dressing:
1 tablespoon lime juice
2 tablespoons extra virgin olive oil
iodized sea salt

Mix all the ingredients in a big bowl. Drizzle with lime juice and olive oil. Sprinkle with sea salt and serve with tostones or arepas.

Serves 4 cups
1 cup = 220 calories

Hen Salad (v)

Hen salad is often served at birthday parties and holidays. It's usually served with mayo, here's my much healthier version.

Preparation and cooking time: 50 minutes

4 organic free range boneless, skinless hen or chicken breasts (discard for vegetarian)
1 onion, peeled and cut into 2 pieces
3 medium sized organic potatoes, steamed or roasted
3 medium sized organic carrots, steamed or roasted
3 organic free range hard boiled eggs
2 cups frozen or fresh peas, cooked

dressing:
1 cup organic plain yogurt
¼ cup extra-virgin olive oil
1 tablespoon organic Worcestershire sauce
1 tablespoon apple cider vinegar
1 teaspoon mustard
2 teaspoons organic honey
1 teaspoons iodized sea salt
pinch white pepper

Boil or steam breasts for 25 minutes adding the onion to the water before it starts to boil. Remove chicken breasts and set aside to cool. Discard onion. (skip this process for a vegetarian option). Peel and chop potatoes and carrots, chop eggs and add them to a large bowl.

Shred the breasts with a fork or by hand. Add the breasts to the potato mixture and add the peas. In a medium bowl, whisk yogurt with olive oil, Worcestershire sauce, apple cider vinegar, mustard, honey, sea salt and pepper. Pour the dressing over chicken salad and mix well. Refrigerate for 2 hours before serving.

Makes 8-10 portions
1 cup = 260 calories

Russian Salad (v)

Yes, we have our own version of the famous Russian Salad. The recipe was brought over by the Spaniards and spread all over South America. Created by Lucien Olivier Guillerminav in 1860, as the head chef of the Hermitage restaurant in Moscow. Also called "Olivier Salad", is so traditional that we forget that it is really Russian. Some people make it at home on a weekly basis and it's served in most Venezuelan restaurants too.

Preparation and cooking time: 1 hour

1 medium organic beet
1 medium organic potato
2 medium organic carrots
extra-virgin olive oil
2 organic cage free hard boiled eggs, peeled
dressing:
1 cup organic plain yogurt
1 teaspoon mustard
1 tablespoon lemon juice
1 teaspoon extra virgin olive oil
1 teaspoon apple cider vinegar
pinch of tabasco sauce
$\frac{1}{2}$ teaspoon iodized sea salt
$\frac{1}{2}$ teaspoon organic honey

Preheat oven at 400 F.
Coat beet and potato with olive oil. Place beet and potato on a baking sheet and roast for 45 minutes, let cool. Meanwhile, coat carrots with olive oil and roast for 30 minutes, let cool. Peel and chop beet, potato and carrots, set aside.

Chop eggs and in a medium sized bowl, mix with potato, beet and carrots. In a separate bowl, mix yogurt, mustard, lemon juice, olive oil, apple cider vinegar, tabasco sauce, sea salt and honey. Add to the salad and mix gently. Refrigerate for 2 hours before serving.

Serves 3-4 cups
1 cup = 220 calories

SAUCES

Garlic Sauce (v)

This sauce is very popular in Venezuelan fast food joints. You can pour it on hot dogs, hamburgers, pepitos and fried arepas called " tostadas ".

Preparation time: 5-10 minutes

1 cup organic plain yogurt (substitute with coconut yogurt for vegan)
2 teaspoons garlic paste
1 tablespoon lemon juice
1 tablespoon mustard
pinch tabasco sauce
large pinch onion powder
1 tablespoon organic Worcestershire sauce
$\frac{1}{4}$ organic green pepper
1 tablespoon extra-virgin olive oil
$\frac{1}{2}$ teaspoon organic honey
iodized sea salt
1 tablespoon organic cilantro or parsley

Clean, devein and cut green pepper into pieces. Add each ingredient into a blender and run on high until smooth, about 1-2 minutes.

Serves 1 cup
1 tablespoon = 33 calories

German Sauce (v)

There's a town in Venezuela called " Colonia Tovar " (Tovar Colony). Founded in 1843 by Catholic settlers from south Germany, it's surrounded by mountains and located 26 miles away from Caracas, the capital.

There are many places selling organic strawberry preserves as well as homemade sausages and tartar sauces in this town. Venezuelans make a lighter take on tartar sauce and it's available in fast food joints, food trucks and hot dog carts.

Preparation time: 10-15 minutes

½ cup organic plain yogurt (substitute with coconut yogurt for vegan)
1 teaspoon mustard
1 tablespoon fresh lemon juice
1 tablespoon organic Worcestershire sauce
1 tablespoon extra-virgin olive oil
pinch of tabasco sauce
½ teaspoon iodized sea salt
½ teaspoon organic honey
1 tablespoon onion, finely chopped
1 tablespoon organic parsley, chopped
½ tablespoon capers in salt, rinsed and finely chopped

Mix all the ingredients in a medium sized bowl and refrigerate for 1 hour before serving. Use a squeeze bottle for best results.

Serves ¾ cup
¼ cup = 75 calories

Green Sauce (v)

Capers are best preserved in salt, make sure to use these instead of the vinegar marinated ones. This sauce can be used on steaks, chicken and fish.

Preparation time: 15 minutes

1 cup organic parsley
3 garlic cloves or 1 teaspoon garlic paste
2 teaspoons anchovy paste
2 teaspoons capers, rinsed
½ cup extra virgin olive oil
1 tablespoon fresh lemon juice

Blend all ingredients on high until smooth and refrigerate for 1 hour before serving.

Serves ¾ cup

1 teaspoon = 30 calories

Guasacaca (gwa. sa. Ka. kah.) (v)

This is the original sauce found in restaurants. It's chunky, acidic and a delicious compliment for steaks, rotisserie chickens, arepas and empanadas. At home, people add avocados and tomatoes. I've made it an option to choose between the restaurant style and the homemade style.

Preparation time: 15 minutes

2 tablespoons organic fresh cilantro
2 tablespoons organic fresh parsley
1 organic green bell pepper, seeded and cut into chunks
1 medium onion, cut into chunks
4 garlic cloves, peeled
$\frac{1}{2}$ cup white wine vinegar
$\frac{1}{2}$ cup filtered water
$\frac{1}{4}$ cup extra virgin olive oil (discard for a clear, fat free version)
$\frac{1}{2}$ teaspoon iodized sea salt

1-2 organic green or red tomatoes, cut into chunks (optional)
1 avocado, peeled and cut into chunks (optional)

Rinse cilantro and parsley, cut off stems. Blend all the ingredients on medium or low for 1 minute, leaving the sauce chunky.
Refrigerate for 24 hours before serving.

Makes 2 $\frac{1}{2}$ cups
$\frac{1}{2}$ cup = 43 calories

Picante Pickled Sauce
(pee. Kan. Taeh) (v)

Pre - Columbian Indigenous tribes used hot and sweet peppers in their daily meals. Venezuelan Amazon natives would use the leftover water from boiled yuca as their liquid to make their " picante " pickled sauce. There are other variations, from milk, latin sour cream and vinegar based. It was originally used on fish, for its digestive and sensual powers, but now its poured on anything from soups, stews, arepas and steaks.

*You will need a medium sized pickle jar with a glass lid for these recipes.

Preparation time: 15 minutes

Yogurt based Picante Sauce:
½ cup organic whole milk
½ cup organic plain yogurt
½ teaspoon iodized sea salt
4 organic sweet peppers, cut in half (various colors)
6 organic hot peppers, cut in half (various colors)
4 whole garlic cloves, peeled
1 tablespoon organic cilantro stalks

Whisk milk and yogurt in a medium bowl, add the salt, set aside. Rinse peppers, garlic and cilantro and add them to the jar. Pour the milk-yogurt mixture into the jar. Cover, shake and refrigerate overnight. The longer it stays in the fridge, the stronger and more flavorful it will be.
*Only use the liquid.

Makes 1 cup
1 tablespoon = 14 calories

Preparation time: 15 minutes

Vinegar based Picante Sauce:
4 organic sweet peppers, cut in half (various colors)
6 organic hot peppers, cut in half (various colors)
4 whole garlic cloves, peeled
1 small onion, cut into 4 pieces
1 tablespoon organic cilantro stalks
pepper
½ teaspoon iodized sea salt
1 cup white wine vinegar or apple cider vinegar (substitute with vodka for maximum potency)
¼ cup extra virgin olive oil

 Rinse the peppers and add to the jar. Add the rest of the ingredients, one by one. Close and shake jar to mix well. Refrigerate overnight.
*Only use the liquid.

Makes 1 ¼ cups
1 teaspoon = 10 calories

Pink Sauce (v)

This rose sauce is another favorite in fast food joints. It's basically mayo, ketchup and a little mustard. You can make your own with healthier ingredients.

Preparation time: 15 minutes

1 cup organic plain yogurt (substitute with coconut yogurt for vegan)
1 ½ tablespoons organic tomato paste
¼ teaspoon allspice
½ teaspoon onion powder
½ teaspoon garlic paste
1 teaspoon organic honey
1 teaspoon organic apple cider vinegar
iodized sea salt
1 teaspoon mustard
1 tablespoon fresh lemon juice
pinch tobasco sauce or paprika
¼ cup extra virgin olive oil

Whisk all the ingredients one by one in a medium bowl. Sauce should be pink. Refrigerate for 1 hour before serving.

Makes 1 ¼ cups
1 tablespoon = 40 calories

Sofrito (so. Free. Toh) (v)

This is a base sauce we use for stews, soups and beans. Used in Spain, Portugal and Latin America, sofrito is cooked separately and added right before a soup or stew is ready to thicken and add flavor.

Cooking time: 20 minutes

1-2 tablespoons annatto colored extra virgin olive oil
1 onion, finely chopped
2 cloves garlic, minced
$\frac{1}{2}$ organic green pepper, seeded and finely chopped
1 organic sweet pepper, seeded and finely chopped
2 organic tomatoes, chopped
1 teaspoon organic Worcestershire sauce
pinch ground cumin
iodized sea salt
$\frac{1}{4}$ cup filtered water

Heat olive oil over medium heat, add onion, garlic and peppers. Cook until soft, about 5 minutes, and add the tomatoes, Worcestershire sauce, cumin and salt. Stir to mix well.

Add the water, simmer until all the ingredients blend in, about 10-15 minutes. At this point it can be added to anything you wish or let cool. Refrigerate in an air tight container and used when needed.

Serves 1 cup
$\frac{1}{4}$ cup = 84 calories

Venezuelan Criolla Sauce (v)

This raw, light, mild and fresh summery sauce can be used on steaks, chicken, fish, tostones, arepas, and almost anything you can think of.

Preparation time: 15 minutes

1 medium onion, finely chopped
2 organic tomatoes, finely chopped
2 tablespoons organic cilantro, finely chopped
¼ cup extra virgin olive oil
1 tablespoon apple cider vinegar
iodized sea salt
pepper

Mix all the ingredients in a medium bowl. Refrigerate for 1 hour before serving.

Makes 2 cups
¼ cup = 50 calories

SOUPS

Asparagus Cream Soup (v)

Asparagus is very high in vitamin K among other vitamins and minerals. Is better to eat asparagus with fat (olive oil, butter, coconut oil) for better absorption of this vitamin as it is fat soluble. Bugs don't like asparagus so there's no need to buy organic as they don't have any pesticides on them. There are many instant asparagus cream soups out there. I used to love eating them as a kid in Venezuela. But home-made versions are way healthier, without msg, high fructose corn syrup, etc.

Cooking time: 40 minutes

1 asparagus bunch
extra virgin olive oil
iodized sea salt
pepper
2 tablespoons organic butter
1 onion, chopped
½ teaspoon garlic paste
2 cups organic low sodium vegetable broth
1 cup organic plain yogurt
1 tablespoon fresh lemon juice

Preheat oven at 400 F.
Rinse asparagus and pat dry with paper towel. Discard hard bottom ends by braking them off with your hands and chop the rest. Place asparagus on a baking dish, sprinkle olive oil, salt and pepper and roast for 15 min. Take out from oven and let stand.

Heat butter over medium heat, add onion and garlic. Cook until soft, about 5 minutes. Add asparagus and broth, simmer for 10 minutes.
In a bowl, whisk ½ cup of hot broth from the asparagus into yogurt. Slowly, whisk the yogurt to the asparagus, add lemon juice. Cook on medium-low heat for 10 minutes. Remove from heat and blend. Return to pot and let stand for 5 minutes. Adjust salt and pepper if needed.

Serves 3 ½ cups
1 cup = 180 calories

Avocado Cream Soup (v)

The rich, creaminess of an avocado is not only considered a good source of healthy fat, it's high in fiber, contains vitamin c, vitamin b-6, magnesium and potassium as well as protein, iron and vitamin a. Here's a recipe for avocado and soup lovers alike.

Cooking time: 18 minutes

2 ripe avocados, peeled and mashed
2 cups organic low-sodium vegetable broth
½ cup organic plain yogurt
1 tablespoon corn flour P.A.N. (substitute with organic coconut flour for gluten free)
1 cup organic whole milk or coconut milk
iodized sea salt
white pepper

Mix the avocado with the broth in a medium pot and simmer over medium heat for 8 minutes. In a small bowl, whisk ¼ cup of hot broth into the yogurt.

Dissolve the corn flour in the yogurt mixture. Whisking slowly, add the milk to the yogurt mixture and pour over the avocado broth, stirring constantly until smooth.

Add the salt and pepper. Cook for 5 minutes over low heat. At this point you may choose to blend the soup for a creamier consistency. Serve hot.

Makes 3 ½ cups
1 cup = 170 calories

Fosforera (phos. pho. Rea. Rah)

This is a soup typically made in the Venezuelan Caribbean Island of Margarita. It's believed to be an aphrodisiac, made with freshly caught fish and seafood.

Cooking time: 1hr and 45 minutes

For the broth:
6 cups seafood stock
2 fish heads
2 organic celery stalks, cut into chunks
2 organic carrots, cut into chunks
1 onion, cut in half
3-4 organic cilantro stalks

For the sofrito:
2 tablespoons extra virgin olive oil
1 tablespoon organic butter
1 onion, finely chopped
2 organic scallions, finely chopped
2 teaspoons garlic paste
½ organic red pepper, seeded and finely chopped
1 organic tomato, chopped
½ cup dry white wine
iodized sea salt
½ lb clams, cleaned
½ lb mussels, cleaned
1 lb calamari, cleaned and cut crosswise
1 lb shrimp, peeled and deveined
1 lb fish fillet (mahi-mahi, red snapper, grouper, etc) with skin and cut crosswise
1-2 tablespoons organic cilantro, chopped

In a large pot, add the water and rest of the ingredients for the broth and simmer over medium-high heat for 1 hour. Discard vegetables by pouring broth through a colander into a bowl. Pour broth back to the pot and keep warm. In a medium sized pan, heat the olive oil and butter over medium heat. Saute onion, scallions, garlic, red pepper, and tomatoes, cook until soft, about 10 minutes. Add white wine and sea salt. Simmer until sofrito thickens, about 10 minutes.

Add calamari, clams and mussels to the sofrito and cook for 10 minutes. Pour the sofrito into the warm broth, simmer for 10 minutes. Remove from heat, add shrimp, fish and let stand for 5 minutes. Sprinkle cilantro and serve with lime wedges.

Makes 6 cups
1 cup = 150 calories

Green Plantain Soup (v)

Rich in complex carbohydrates and low in glycemic index, plantains contain iron, phosphorus, potassium, calcium, magnesium, vitamins B and C. Plantain helps maintain a healthy immune system, skin elasticity, night vision and decrease premenstrual syndrome.

Green plantain soup is used as an astringent for soft stool, treatment and prevention of stomach ulcers. You can either eat it with chunks of plantains or blend it for a more creamy consistency.

Cooking time: 25 minutes

3 tablespoons extra virgin olive oil or organic coconut oil
1 onion, chopped
2 garlic cloves, minced or 1 teaspoon garlic paste
1 small organic green pepper, chopped
1 green plantain, peeled and cut into pieces
4 cups organic vegetable broth
1 tablespoon organic Worcestershire sauce
1 tablespoon organic cilantro, chopped
iodized sea salt

In a medium pot, heat olive oil over medium heat, add the onion, garlic and green pepper, cook until soft, about 5 minutes. Add the plantains and cook for 10 minutes, stirring frequently.

Pour the broth and the Worcestershire sauce into the plantains and simmer on medium-high heat until plantain is soft, about 10 minutes. Add the cilantro and sea salt. At this point you can either serve or blend.

Makes 4 ¼ cups
1 cup = 170 calories

Milk Soup (v)

This is a child friendly soup. I was served this as a child and continue to eat it every once in a while.

The combination of cheese, butter, milk and arepa makes this rich soup a comforting and simple treat bursting with creamy goodness.

Depending on your preference, you can either discard the arepa's crust or add it to the soup.

Cooking time: 15 minutes

¾ cup organic whole milk
1 arepa
1 teaspoon organic butter
2 tablespoons white hard cheese, grated or shredded

Heat milk over medium heat until warm, do not boil. Place warm arepa in a bowl and cut into small pieces.

Pour the warm milk over the arepa, add butter and cheese, mix well to let butter melt and all the flavors combine.

Makes 1 portion
1 portion = 340 calories

Oriental Red Snapper Soup

In the oriental part of Venezuela; Margarita, Cumana or Araya, you will find this nutritious soup loaded with phosphorus in many places...or you can make it at home and enjoy it just the same.

Cooking time: 50 minutes

1 wild caught whole red snapper or any meaty fish, cleaned and sliced
1 lb fish heads (red snapper or other fish), cleaned
iodized sea salt
lime juice
1 onion, julienne style
6 garlic cloves, minced
1 organic green or red pepper, seeded and chopped
4 organic sweet peppers, seeded and chopped
1 organic scallion, sliced
6 cups seafood stock
¼ lb fresh or frozen yuca, peeled
¼ lb yam, peeled and cut into pieces
2 green plantains, peeled and sliced
1 lb pumpkin, cut into pieces
1 tablespoon organic cilantro, chopped
1 cup corn flour (P.A.N.) dough for bollos (optional)
extra virgin olive oil

Rub the fish with sea salt and lime juice. Marinate the fish and fish heads with the onion, garlic, pepper, sweet peppers and scallion. Let stand for 20 minutes. Splash lime juice over plantains.

In a large pot, cook the yuca, yam and plantains in the water until almost ready, about 15 minutes. Separate the fish from the marinade and add the marinade to the yuca mixture, simmer for 20 minutes.

Add the pumpkin, cilantro and bollos, cook for another 10 minutes. Add red snapper and fish heads. Remove from heat and let stand for 5 minutes. Serve with an avocado slice, arepa, and a splash of extra virgin olive oil and lime juice.

Serves 8 portions
1 cup = 150 calories

Pisca Andina (Pees. kah. an. Dee. nah)
(v)

"Andeans awake, letting the rays of the sun silently show the way. Friendly, giving, humble and hard-working, with the frigid cold leaving their cheeks toasted, always in deep contemplation, they admire daily the beauty and wonder of the mountain range of the Andes..."

Pisca Andina is a soup made for breakfast and served with a side of arepas and smoked homemade cheese. It's made with potatoes, chicken broth, eggs, smoked cheese, milk and cilantro. Some add a little spice to it or add a personal touch. If you travel to Merida, Tachira and Trujillo States in Venezuela, you will find this soup, with its delicate, soft and deep cilantro flavor. It will caress your palate and its warmth will surely reach your soul.

Cooking time: 40 minutes

6 cups organic, free range, low sodium chicken broth (use vegetable broth for a vegetarian option)
1 organic potato, peeled and cut into small pieces
2 tablespoons organic butter
1 onion, chopped
2 garlic cloves, minced or ½ teaspoon garlic paste
1 organic scallion, finely chopped
½ organic green pepper, finely chopped
½ cup organic plain yogurt
iodized sea salt
½ cup organic cilantro, chopped
4 organic free range eggs
¼ lb crumbled fresh feta cheese or hard white cheese

In a medium pot, cook potatoes in the broth over medium-high heat until soft, about 15 minutes, turn heat to medium-low and keep warm. In a separate sauce pan, heat butter and add onion, garlic, scallion and green pepper, cook over medium heat until soft, about 5-10 minutes.

Pour onion "sofrito" over potato-broth. Slowly, add ½ cup hot broth to yogurt in a small bowl, stirring constantly. Whisking constantly, add yogurt mixture to soup. Sprinkle with sea salt and add cilantro, stir and cook over low heat for 5 minutes.

Add the eggs, one by one, in a separate space in the soup, making sure the yolk doesn't break. Remove from heat and cover. Let it stand for 5-10 minutes or until eggs are poached. Sprinkle with cheese and serve with arepas.

Serves 6 cups
1 cup = 350 calories

Pumpkin Soup (v)

This scrumptious soup is made with green peppers and ground cumin, adding a deep " sabor latino ", giving it a very distinctive and unique taste.

Cooking time: 30 minutes

4 cups organic vegetable broth
2 lb pumpkin, peeled and cut into cubes
1 tablespoons extra virgin olive oil
1 tablespoon organic butter
1 onion, chopped
1 organic red pepper, chopped
½ teaspoon ground cumin
large pinch ground nutmeg
large pinch white pepper
iodized sea salt
1 tablespoon organic cilantro, chopped
organic plain yogurt

Cook pumpkin in vegetable broth until soft, about 20 minutes. A fork should be able to go through the pieces easily. Heat olive oil and butter over medium heat. Saute onion and red pepper until soft, about 5 minutes.

Add the onion sofrito, cumin, nutmeg, white pepper, salt and cilantro. Stir and cook for 5 minutes. Blend the pumpkin soup and serve with a spoonful of yogurt.

Makes 4 cups
1 cup = 145 calories

Sancocho (san. Koh. cho.) (v)

This soup, also called " hervido ", was served almost daily before the main course during colonial times in Caracas. The broth was made first and then a " sofrito " was added to give it aroma and flavor. Then the broth, the meat or poultry and vegetables were served in 3 different plates. Letting the person pick and choose what they wanted to add to their broth. It can be made as a " cruzao ", a cross from two or more types of meat. In different parts of the country, sancocho is prepared according to the customs and harvest of the region: In the oriental part is prepared mostly with fish. In the central region is meat or hen based and in the andes and plains can also be made with chicken. In the andes region they tend to add green plantains, making it darker. In the plains they make a variation of it by adding rice. And like our indigenous ancestors, some people still use wooden stoves and clay pots, which makes this robust soup obtain a light smoky flavor.

It is believed that this soup can lift the spirit of even the most depressed, sooth any suffering and comfort the ill. This soup is part of our mestizo heritage, beautiful example of our diverse colors and transformation of the products of a rich and abundant land.

Cooking time: 45-50 minutes

12 cups filtered water (substitute with vegetable broth for vegetarian)
½ organic free range chicken, skinned and cut into pieces (discard for vegetarian)
1 organic red pepper, seeded and cut into 2 pieces
½ lb or 4 organic carrots, peeled and cut into small pieces
iodized sea salt to taste
½ lb yam, peeled and cut into cubes
½ lb or 4 organic celery stalks, cleaned and cut into small pieces
1 lb yuca, peeled (the frozen type is already peeled and cooks faster than the fresh one)
4 corns, cut in 2 pieces each
1 lb pumpkin, peeled and cut into cubes

2-3 garlic cloves, minced or 1 tsp crushed garlic
1 onion, chopped
3 organic sweet peppers, chopped
2 tablespoon annatto flavored olive oil
2 tablespoons organic cilantro
lime juice (optional)

In a large pot, add water, chicken, red pepper, carrots and salt. In Venezuela, corn takes a long time to cook as opposed to the US where the corn is very tender and cooks rapidly. If you're using U.S. Corn, add it with the pumpkin, otherwise, add it in the beginning with the chicken.

Cook on medium-high heat until the chicken is tender, about 15-20 minutes. Scoop off the dark foam accumulated on the surface (this is a bad form of protein). Discard the red pepper. Add the yam and celery. Cook until soft, about 10 minutes. Add the yuca, corn and pumpkin.

Meanwhile, make a "sofrito " with the garlic, onion, sweet peppers and annatto olive oil. Add the sofrito and cilantro to the sancocho. Cook until yuca, pumpkin and corn are soft and a fork goes through easily, about 15 minutes. Serve with arepas in medium sized bowls and a splash of lime juice if desired.

Makes 8-10 cups
1 cup = 350 calories

SPREADS, FILLINGS & DIPS

Caraotas (ka. ra. o. tah) (v)
Black Beans

We're the only ones who call black beans " caraotas ". I always have to translate to my fellow Latinos who aren't Venezuelans. This is my mom's recipe, as she always prefers to have the onion-garlic flavor in the oil instead of seeing and chewing on onion and garlic chunks. If you're watching your fat intake, you can always substitute the oil with broth.

Cooking time: 30 minutes

2 tablespoons extra virgin olive oil
1 small onion, chopped
2 garlic cloves, minced
1 can organic black beans
$\frac{1}{4}$ cup filtered water (some beans might need more water)
iodized sea salt
1 tablespoon organic cilantro, finely chopped

Saute the onion and the garlic in olive oil over medium-low heat, until the onion mixture or " sofrito " is soft, about 5 minutes. Place beans in a small pot, add water and let it simmer on medium-high for about 15 minutes.

When beans are almost done, drain the sofrito oil through a colander into the beans and discard onion-garlic mixture. Add salt, cook over medium-low heat until thick., about 5-10 minutes longer. Remove from heat and sprinkle with cilantro.

Serves 2 cups
1 cup = 227 calories

*The basic fillings for arepas are butter and cheese. Here are some suggestions: Whipped butter has half the calories as regular butter (1 tablespoon = 65 calories). Make sure is organic.

Feta cheese (3 tablespoons = 54 calories)
Hard white cheese (3 tablespoons = 52 calories)
Sharp cheddar (2 tablespoon = 74 calories)
Venezuelan " Natilla " or " Suero " are very similar to Mexican and Central American creams which are available in many Latin stores.

Cazon (kah. Son) or (kah. Thon)
Baby Shark

I use annatto in this recipe for coloring. It's the South American version of saffron as it gives the food a yellowish color and a very subtle, but distinctive flavor. Latinos use it on pretty much anything from rice, fish, chicken and soups.

Cooking time: 23 minutes

1 teaspoon annatto seeds
1 tablespoon extra-virgin olive oil
1 lb cazon (baby shark, cod, Pollock or any flaky fish)
filtered water
1 onion, finely chopped
3 garlic cloves, minced
1 organic tomato, chopped (optional)
iodized sea salt

In a small pot, heat the annatto seeds in the olive oil over medium-low heat until it begins to color, about 3 minutes. Once the oil is red, remove from heat and let cool, discard seeds.

Rinse and chop the fish into small chunks. Boil for 5 minutes in enough water to cover, remove from heat and reserve water. Let stand and shred the fish with a fork or by hand when it's cool enough to handle.

Saute the onion and garlic in the annatto infused olive oil until soft, about 5 minutes. Add fish and stir. Add the tomato, some of the fish broth, about ¼ cup, and the sea salt. Cook over medium heat until it's dry, about 5-10 minutes.

Serves 3 cups
½ cup = 240 calories

*Cazon can be used as an empanada or arepa filling and it can also be served with rice

Chicken Liver Pate

My dad and I used to eat the processed pork liver pate from the supermarket with arepas at home. Here's a homemade healthy version with chicken livers instead. Spread it on your warm arepas or bread, together with butter, cheese and eggs.

Cooking time: 18 minutes

4 tablespoons organic butter, plus 4 tablespoons organic raw coconut oil
1 onion, chopped
1 lb organic free range chicken livers
pinch allspice
½ teaspoon iodized sea salt
½ teaspoon maple syrup
1 tablespoon red wine
1 tablespoon organic plain yogurt
pinch pepper

Heat the butter and coconut oil in a medium sauce pan, saute onion until soft, about 5 minutes. Add the chicken livers, allspice, salt and maple syrup, stir.

Cook over medium heat until the livers are slightly brown on the outside but still pink on the inside, about 3-5 minutes. Remove from heat.

Let the chicken livers cool for 5 minutes. Add onion-chicken to a blender and reserve the butter/coconut oil. Blend with red wine, yogurt, and pepper until smooth. Pour in container and add the butter-oil left on the pan on top to seal. Refrigerate for 2-3 hours before serving.

Serves 2 cups aprox
1 tablespoon = 55 calories

Mashed Avocado (v)

Classified as a berry, avocado is a fruit which grows on trees native of Mexico, Central and South America. Venezuelan avocados are fruity and light, while Hass, being the most commercialized in the U.S, is deep, rich and buttery. Avocados are ready to eat when they are slightly soft at the bottom and yield to gentle pressure.

During the 1700's, European sailors used avocados as a spread for biscuits, which led to the name "midshipman's butter".

The Aztecs called the fruit " aoacatl ", which was later translated to " ahuacatl ". In some South American countries it's called " palta ", the name originally given by the Incas.

In Venezuela is called " aguacate " (agoo. ah. kah. teh)

Preparation time: 15 minutes

1 hass avocado
1 tablespoon organic plain yogurt or Mexican cream (optional)
2 tablespoons grated hard white Mexican cheese or crumbled fresh feta cheese

Rinse avocado. Slice it in half by sliding he knife from the top end all the way down and up again to the other side of the top end. Scoop with a spoon, discard peel and seed. Chop avocado.

In a small bowl, mix the avocado and yogurt. Grate cheese and add to avocado mixture. Mash with a fork until you make a paste. Use it as a spread over buttery arepas.

Serves 1 cup
$\frac{1}{4}$ cup = 82 calories

*Store leftovers in an air tight container, splashing lime juice over it to avoid browning.

Perico (peˈ ɾi. ko) (v)

This is a common Venezuelan breakfast eggs. The word " perico " means many things in Venezuela; a person who talks too much, a type of bird and even a type of drug. But we're going to focus on the type of food in this book.

Cooking time: 35 minutes

1 tablespoon extra-virgin olive oil
1 small onion, finely chopped
3 organic tomatoes, chopped
¼ cup filtered water
4 organic eggs or 5 egg whites, lightly beaten
iodized sea salt
1 teaspoon organic cilantro, chopped (optional)

In a medium saucepan, heat olive oil over medium high heat. Add the onion, cook until lightly brown and caramelized, about 10 minutes.

Add the tomatoes and the water, simmer until the tomatoes are blended with the onion in a thick sauce, about 15 minutes. Sprinkle with sea salt.

Add the eggs, stir and mix well, heat until eggs are cooked through, and sauce is on the dry side, about 10 minutes more. Sprinkle with cilantro, stir and serve with arepas.

Makes 2-3 portions
½ cup = 115 calories

*The perico picture included was made with egg whites

Reina Pepiada (rej.na pe.pee.a.tha)
Curvy Queen

This particular filling was invented in honor of a beauty queen. Susana Duijm was representing Venezuela when she won the Miss World crown in 1955. And back in the day curvy women were the most desired. The base for this recipe is chicken, avocado and peas. It should be served at room temperature. There are many variations, but this is a guilt free one.

Cooking time: 30 minutes

1 organic boneless and skinless chicken breast
filtered water
1 onion, cut in 4 pieces
2 garlic cloves
$\frac{1}{2}$ organic red pepper, cut in 4 pieces (optional)
iodized sea salt

$\frac{1}{4}$ cup organic plain yogurt
1 teaspoon mustard
1 tablespoon lemon juice
1 teaspoon extra virgin olive oil
1 tablespoon organic Worcestershire sauce
pinch of tabasco sauce
pinch iodized sea salt

$\frac{1}{4}$ cup fresh or frozen peas, cooked
1 small onion, finely chopped
1 organic leaf lettuce
$\frac{1}{4}$ avocado, sliced

Boil the chicken breast in the water together with the onion, garlic red pepper and salt until soft, about 20 minutes. Drain, discard onion and garlic. Let cool for 5 minutes. Shred the chicken with a fork or by hand, set aside.

In a bowl, mix yogurt, mustard, lemon juice, olive oil, Worcestershire sauce, tabasco, sea salt, peas and the chopped onion. Add the shredded chicken and mix well.

Fill arepa with the lettuce, then the chicken mixture and top with the sliced avocado.

Serves 2 generous arepa fillings

½ cup = 220 calories

*You may choose to grill or bake the chicken breast instead; 10 minutes on each side on a grilling pan and 10 minutes on each side for baking, with a preheated oven at 400 F.

Sardines and Tomato Dip

Sardines are named after Sardinia, the Italian island where large schools of these fish were once found. Napoleon Bonaparte initiated the canning of sardines, the first fish ever to be canned. Sardines are a rich source of omega-3 fatty acids, vitamin d, vitamin b-12, iron and because they are small fish and at the bottom of the food chain, they are not as likely to have concentrated amounts of mercury and other contaminants.

Here's a funny anecdote:
Long time ago, while I was living in New Orleans with my mom. My dad was living and working in Venezuela and one day while he was at work, some robbers broke into our house, they took a few things, but the funny part was that they had enough time to sit and eat my dad's favorite canned sardines with crackers and all ! I think he resented that the most.

This treat can be served as a filling for arepas or as a canape with crackers. Canned fish is better preserved in oil, so avoid the water based ones.

Preparation time: 10 minutes

1 can sardines in olive oil
1 organic tomato, chopped
1 tablespoon lime juice
pinch iodized sea salt

Clean scales off the sardines with the back of a small knife and slice each sardine lengthwise in half by making a cut from front to back in the bottom part of the fish, discard the vertebrae (see picture).

In a small bowl, mix the sardines with the tomato, lime juice and sea salt. Stir with a fork.

Serves 1-2 arepa filling
½ cup = 97 calories

Tomatada (to. ma. Ta. Tha) (v)
Tomato Stew

Tomato is a berry fruit but considered a vegetable for culinary purposes. Native of the South American Andes, it was first used as food in Mexico. The Aztecs and other people in Mesoamerica used the fruit in their cooking. The Pueblo people are thought to believe that those who witnessed the ingestion of tomato seeds were blessed with powers of divination.

It contains lycopene, one of the most powerful natural antioxidants. Research have shown that tomatoes can protect against sunburn and help keep skin looking youthful. Tomato consumption has been associated with decrease risk of breast cancer and might be protective against neurodegenerative diseases. Its consumption might be beneficial for reducing cardiovascular risk associated with type 2 diabetes.

They are widely used in Mediterranean and South American diets. The acidity and sweetness of the tomato mixed with a buttery arepa makes this one of my favorite delectable dips.

Cooking time: 20 minutes

1 tablespoon extra virgin olive oil
2 organic tomatoes, chopped
1 small onion, chopped (optional)
2 slices organic uncured ham, chopped (optional)
iodized sea salt
water

If you're using onions, saute in 1 tablespoon of olive oil until soft. Add the tomatoes and water.

Heat to boil, reduce heat to medium low, add salt. Mash the tomatoes with a fork and cook until the tomatoes are soft and turns into a thick, chunky sauce. Add the ham towards the end and stir.

Serves 1 cup
1 cup (tomato only) = 40 calories

Tuna Dip

The taste of summer explodes with the contrast between the cold acidity of this fresh filling and the warm sweetness of a buttery arepa.

Preparation time: 15 minutes

1 can tuna in olive oil (tuna preserves best in olive oil)
1 small onion, finely chopped
2 organic tomatoes, chopped
1 tablespoon fresh lime juice
pinch iodized sea salt
1 tablespoon organic fresh cilantro, chopped

In a medium bowl, mix the tuna with the rest of the ingredients and stir with a fork. Serve at room temperature or cold.

Serves 2-3 fillings
$\frac{1}{2}$ cup = 178 calories

*You can substitute with fresh tuna, by steaming or boiling ¼ lb fresh tuna fillet for 5-10 minutes and letting it cool before shredding and adding it to the rest of the ingredients.

STREET FOOD

Hot Dogs (v)

There are hot dog stands all over Venezuela. The best tasting ones are the small wiener hot dogs. Every topping is fresh and homemade.

Preparation and cooking time: 25 minutes

1 organic beef, turkey, chicken or vegetarian wiener
1 tablespoon extra-virgin olive oil
1 whole grain gluten free hot dog bun
1 tablespoon onion, finely chopped
1 tablespoon cabbage salad, without dressing
1 tablespoon canned or frozen corn, drained
1 tablespoon pink sauce or garlic sauce
mustard (optional)
1 teaspoon grated parmesan or pecorino cheese

Grill, or saute wiener in olive oil for 5 minutes, turning over making sure all sides are slightly browned and caramelized.

Meanwhile, toast bread in toaster oven for 3 minutes. Put wiener in between bun and sprinkle onion, cabbage salad, corn, sauce and cheese on top.

Serves 1
1 hot dog = 280 calories

Patacones (pah. ttah. Koh. ness.) (v)
Plantain sandwiches

Patacones are served mostly in the Zulia State, located on the north west frontier from Colombia. Its origin goes back to the Colombian migration to Venezuela. There are many variations, but it's basically a plantain sandwich filled with a salad, beef or chicken, cheese and sauce. It can be made with green or ripe plantains. You can make it vegetarian by discarding the beef or chicken and substituting with cooked beans. This is a recipe for one big sandwich.

Preparation and cooking time: 15-20 minutes

1 plantain, green or ripe
2-3 tablespoons extra virgin coconut oil
shredded white Mexican, sliced fresh mozzarella or feta cheese
$\frac{1}{2}$ cup organic cooked shredded beef or chicken (substitute with cooked beans for vegetarian)
1-2 organic leaf lettuce
1 organic tomato, sliced
iodized sea salt
garlic, German, guasacaca or pink sauce
sliced avocado (optional)

Cut the ends off from the plantain, peel and cut into two pieces. Pan-fry the plantain on both sides in the coconut oil, for 1 minute on each side (skip this step if plantain is ripe).

Place one by one in between 2 wooden cutting boards and press down until plantain is flat. Sprinkle a little salt on both sides of the patacones. Pan-fry them again in coconut oil for 1 minute on each side. Drain any excess oil on a paper towel.

Place a patacon slice on a plate, add the cheese, shredded beef, chicken or beans, sliced tomato, lettuce, avocado and sauce, topped with the second patacon on top and you have a plantain sandwich.

Serves 1 sandwich
1 sandwich = 270 calories

Peanut Burgers

You can try different types of nuts with this recipe, but if you're allergic to nuts, you can use sunflower seeds instead. It will taste just as good.

Preparation and cooking time: 1 h and 25 minutes

$\frac{1}{2}$ lb grass-fed ground beef
1 small onion, finely chopped or blended
1 teaspoon garlic paste
2 tablespoons roasted peanuts, crushed
2 organic free range egg yolks
iodized sea salt
pepper
$\frac{1}{2}$ teaspoon garlic powder (optional)
1 teaspoon cumin powder
1 teaspoon oregano

Marinade:
$\frac{1}{4}$ cup organic beef broth
1 tablespoon organic Worcestershire sauce
1 tablespoon fresh lemon juice
1 teaspoon tabasco sauce

Rinse ground beef with water in a colander and drain. Place beef in a bowl and combine with the rest of the ingredients. Roll a ball and make the beef patties.

Mix all the marinade ingredients and place in a ziploc bag and add the beef patties. Leave in the fridge for 1 hour. Broil or grill for 5 minutes on each side for medium burgers.

Place burger on a previously toasted, whole wheat or whole grain gluten free burger bun. Add sliced cheddar cheese, 1 tablespoon of each: chopped onions, cabbage salad, canned corn (drained), pink and/or garlic sauce and grated parmesan cheese.

Serves 2 thick patties
1 peanut burger = 320 calories

Pepito (peh. Pee. toh)

There seems to be many pepito recipes out there, but the one I like the most is the one from my home town in Valencia, Venezuela. There's a street called " calle del hambre " (hunger street) where people go after a night out at bars and clubs. You would see rows of junk food joints one after another serving hot dogs, hamburgers and pepitos among others. The best was the high-protein " con todo " (with everything) pepito. Here it is...

Preparation and cooking time: 25 minutes

2 whole grain gluten free baguettes
1 tablespoon extra-virgin olive oil
1 onion, sliced crosswise
½ lb grass-fed sirloin steak, sliced and/or ½ cage free chicken breast, thinly sliced
½ teaspoon cumin
iodized sea salt
pepper
4 strips uncured organic bacon or turkey bacon, cut into small pieces
1 tablespoon organic Worcestershire sauce
4 slices uncured organic ham or turkey, cut into small pieces
2 tablespoons cabbage salad (no dressing)
2 tablespoons canned kernel corn
1-2 tablespoons guasacaca, pink, German and/or garlic sauce

Saute the onion in a medium sauce pan over medium heat in the olive oil until soft, about 5 minutes. Add the steak and/or chicken. Sprinkle with cumin, sea salt and pepper.

Add the bacon and cook until onion, steak and bacon are browned and caramelized. Add the Worcestershire sauce and ham, cook for 5 minutes. Remove from heat.

Heat baguettes in a toaster oven for 3 minutes. Place the steak mixture on the baguettes and add cabbage salad, canned corn and sauces.

Serves 2 pepitos
1 pepito = 380 calories

Venezuelan Staples

Arepas (a ' Reh. Pah) (v)

Most Venezuelans eat arepas on a daily basis; for breakfast, lunch and dinner. It can either be served plain as bread with the main course, a side for soups, salads or as a sandwich with many different fillings. Arepas are made with corn/maize flour, which is very low in gluten. Some people add eggs, milk and even grated cheese to the water for the dough, this recipe is much lighter and vegan.

*Add 1 tablespoon of coarse wheat bran to add fiber to the original recipe (It's gluten free).

Cooking time: 30 minutes

1 cup warm filtered water
1/2 teaspoon iodized sea salt
1 teaspoon organic coconut oil
white maize flour (Harina P.A.N. or Goya Masarepa)

Preheat oven at 400 F.

Mix water, sea salt, coconut oil in a bowl. Slowly, add the flour while mixing it with your hand until you obtain a slightly sticky dough. Heat a flat pan or griddle over medium heat, spread a little oil over it with a paper towel.

Make a ball from the dough and then flatten it making sure all sides stay as round as possible. You can make it as thin or thick as you like. Wet one of your hands and pat the arepa a bit on both sides. The contrast between the oil on the pan and the water will prevent the arepas from sticking to the pan.

Lay arepas on the pan and brown on both sides, about 5-7 minutes on each side. Place them in the oven for 10-15 minutes. Arepas should be crispy on the outside and soft on the inside. Remove from the oven and stuff with butter and cheese and/or your favorite filling.

Serves 2 medium arepas
1 arepa = 165 calories

*Avoid reheating cold arepas in the microwave, otherwise they will become chewy. Use oven or toaster oven instead, reheat for 10 minutes.

Variations:
  Bollo (Boh. Yo)
Add balls of dough into salted boiling filtered water. Once they come up into the surface, they're done, about 15 min.

  Tostada (tos. Ta. tha)
Saute old arepas filled with ham and/or cheese in 2 tablespoons organic extra virgin coconut oil on both sides until light brown, about 5 min on each side.

Cachapas (ca. Cha. pah) (v)
Corn Cakes

My mom and I never really made this at home, we thought it was too much work. My mom loved to ride just outside the city looking for new outdoorsy spots where cachapas were their specialties. When we would hear about a place where they would add flour to the cachapas, we felt disgusted, never went back and started searching for new places to go, mostly through word of mouth.

*Corn in Venezuela takes longer to cook than in the U.S. It's less tender and less moist too. So, if you're making cachapas in the U.S. It's ok to use a little bit of corn flour, (we won't feel disgusted if you do). I'm not sure about the rest of the world so start with no flour and if you see that the mixture is too moist, then add the corn/maize flour.

Cooking time: 20 minutes

3 yellow corns
1 tablespoon organic turbinado, raw brown sugar
1 teaspoon iodized sea salt
1/3 cup corn flour P.A.N (substitute with gluten free corn or coconut flour)
1 organic, free range egg (substitute 1 tablespoon organic, sugar free, apple sauce)

Hold the corn upward and slice from top to bottom with a knife to take out all the kernels, rotate and continue until you've taken all the kernels out from each corn.

Blend with the rest of the ingredients and let stand for 5 minutes. Pour over a flat, greased hot pan and cook over medium heat until light brown, about 5 minutes on each side.

Spread butter and sprinkle grated hard white cheese, crumbled feta or sliced fresh mozzarella, fold and enjoy.

Serves 2 medium sized cachapas
1 cachapa = 150 calories

Empanadas (em. pah. Nah. Thas) (v)
Turnovers

I used to live half an hour away from the beaches in Puerto Cabello. On the road prior to arriving at the beach there's a spot called " El Palito " (the little stick). Where there were rows on both sides of the street with tons of ladies making empanadas outdoors right from scratch. You could pick and choose which filling was of your liking as they had them on display; grated white cheese, cazon and caraotas. You could watch how they made each empanada and eat them with smoke still flowing out of them as you took the first bite. I used to have at least 3 and maybe take some more to go and eat them sitting by the beach later in the day. I used to drink fresh coconut water and my mom used to get the sweet arepitas. Some restaurants sold fried fresh fish, tostones and fish soups too. Outdoor sittings were available with plastic plates and colorful plastic table cloths together with beer and loud music. My mother loves the beach and we used to go every weekend and on holidays during my childhood and teen years. Here's my old school style inspiration:

Cooking time: 30 minutes

1 cup warm water
pinch olive oil
1 teaspoon iodized sea salt
2 teaspoons organic maple syrup
yellow corn flour (P. A. N.) or Goya yellow corn flour Masarepa
2-3 tablespoons coconut oil
previously cooked filling (black beans, cheese, ground beef, shredded beef or cazon)
1 small bowl, plastic wrap or a piece of a plastic bag, previously washed. (see pictures)

Add olive oil, sea salt, maple syrup and flour to the water in a bowl. Make the dough just like you would for arepas. Place the plastic wrap or bag on a flat counter, rub it with an olive oil moisten paper towel on both sides to make it stick to the counter, this will also prevent the dough from sticking to the bag. Place a ball of the dough in the middle of the plastic, flatten it with the tips of your fingers all around until you have a very thin round layer of dough. Spoon your favorite filling, no more than 3-4 tablespoons, fold empanada in half by placing your hand under the plastic making sure none of the filling comes out and all ends meet making a half-moon.

 Place half of the small bowl following the inside of the half-moon edge of the empanada you just made and press to seal all edges. Take empanada off plastic and saute in coconut oil until lightly browned, about 5 minutes on each side. (Illustrations show step by step process. From left to right and from top to bottom).
Makes 3-4 empanadas, 1 empanada = 230 calories

* If you choose to bake them brush each empanada with coconut oil. Pre heat oven at 400 F and bake for 10 minutes on each side. Serve with guasacaca or tabasco sauce.
**As a safety precaution, make sure all fillings are dry before placing them on the dough. Otherwise, if sauce runs out of the empanada into the oil while frying, the oil will squirt.

Ham Bread

This is the typical homemade bread served during Christmas time in Venezuela. The deep, sour taste of the olives, contrasting with its buttery sweet flavors makes it so satisfyingly unique. It originated back in 1905 in Caracas, by the Ramella Bakery. It was created as a way of using bits and pieces of leftover holiday ham (imported from Spain at the time) sold to customers. The pieces were marinated in spices and wine, rolled in soft dough and baked. Later, olives and raisins were added. Nowadays, people add bacon and a sugar cane glaze to give it a shiny finish and sweet touch. Personally, I can eat this bread daily, all day, and I'm not a bread person !

Preparation and cooking time: 1 hr

Bread:
3 cups William Sonoma's or Thomas Keller's cup 4 cup gluten free flour
½ tablespoon iodized sea salt
1 tablespoon organic maple syrup
½ stick organic salted butter, melted
1 cup organic whole milk
1 organic cage free egg, lightly beaten
Filling:
½ lb (8 oz) organic uncured sliced ham or turkey ham
½ lb (4 oz) organic uncured bacon or turkey bacon
¼ cup raisins
½ cup stuffed olives
1 tablespoon capers in salt, rinsed and drained

Make a circle with the flour and add half the butter (¼ cup / 2 oz) with sea salt and maple syrup in the middle. Knead adding the milk until the dough doesn't stick to your hands. Let stand for 15 minutes.
Extend with a roller into a good rectangle or square. Varnish lightly with the other half of the butter, lay out ham and bacon on the dough. Spread olives, raisins and capers. Roll from one side to the other making sure the ends are sealed and poke holes on it with a fork or a toothpick

Seal and varnish the ends with beaten egg. Let stand for 15 minutes. Bake for 20-25 minutes in a previously heated oven at 400 F until golden brown. Let stand for 15 minutes before serving.

Makes 1 medium bread
1 slice = 200 calories
*Keep refrigerated and heat leftovers in conventional or toaster oven

Pabellon (pa.be o n ˈ ʎ)

" Pabellon Criollo " is a Venezuelan traditional platter which is part of the gastronomy and recognized as the national dish. It's basically consisting of white rice, shredded beef, black beans and fried sweet plantains. Sometimes the beans can be refried and grated hard white cheese can be sprinkled as well. The history of the pabellon dates from colonial times, probably around XVIII century, and by all accounts is a leftover gatherings of previous meals made up by the slaves of haciendas; so the meat, black beans and rice were a day or two old, being the " tajadas " (fried sweet plantains) prepared fresh.

Variations

Here are some variations of the original pabellon:
- Pabellon a caballo (riding pabellon): besides the ingredients mentioned previously, a fried egg is included.
- Pabellon con arepas (with arepas): usually for breakfast, arepas are used instead of rice and sides of avocados with salt and even scrambled eggs are included. Also known as a breakfast pabellon.
- Vegetarian: this kind is made by substituting the shredded beef with eggplant (see recipe).
- Plains: the shredded beef is usually made with different cuts of meat from deer, chiguire or lapa.
- In the west and central plains: sometimes pasta is used instead of rice and fried egg is added too. In this case is called " pabellon alterado " (altered pabellon).
- Margaritan pabellon: sugar is added to the " caraotas " (black beans) in the east and coastal regions and in occasions shredded beef is substituted with fish or seafood prepared the same way. Especially in the Margarita island, where cazon (baby shark) fish is shredded and stewed.
- Lara state: fried goat beef is used instead, this is called " grass hopper foot ".
- Andes and parts of Zulia state: tostones are used instead of sweet plantains.
- Zulia: the shredded beef is cooked with coconut.

Whichever you choose to try, pabellon is a warm, bursting explosion of healthy rich flavors combined to satisfy even the pickiest of eaters.

1 pabellon = 380 calories

Tajadas (ta. Ha. thas.) (v)
Fried Sweet Plantains

My mother told me a story which I don't have much recollection of. It goes back to when I was 2 years old. My parents were getting together with some of my mother's family members at a very fancy restaurant. I was seated on a high chair and everyone was on their best behavior. After everyone looked at the menu, our waiter came over and asked what we wanted to order. At that moment I said in a very loud, firm voice in baby Spanish: " paghetee y ta-ada! " (spaghetty and tajadas). Everyone, including the waiter, burst into laughter, and did I mention it was a steakhouse?... I guess even at a young age I had a passion for not only food, but Italian and Venezuelan alike.

Here's a recipe where I combine the sweet crisp caramel of the ripe fried plantain with the salty contrast of grated white cheese, adding butter to melt all flavors together in a soft bite.

*Use a plantain that is ripe; yellow and half way covered in black or brown spots.

Cooking time: 10 minutes

2-3 tablespoons organic virgin coconut oil
1 ripe plantain
1 teaspoon organic whipped butter
1 tablespoon hard white cheese

Slice the ends off the plantain, discard and cut in half. Use the knife to slightly cut from the top and all the way down the inside curve. Do not go too deep or you'll cut the flesh. Pull the peel off with your hands. You can cut it crosswise or lengthwise. I prefer lengthwise, it cooks much faster and the taste is the same.

Heat coconut oil in a frying pan, when hot, add the plantains. Cook for 1 minute on each side. Use paper towel to soak any extra oil. Spread butter while " tajadas " are hot and let it melt, grate the cheese on top and serve.

Serves 1-2 portions (6 to 8 slices).
1 fried plantain with butter = 150 calories

*You can make a plantain sandwich by putting the " tajadas " between 2 slices of whole wheat or whole grain gluten free bread (see picture).

Variations:
Boiled
 Use plantains that are yellow and have just a bit of black spots. Cut 15-20 minutes, a fork should cut through the plantain easily. Take out of the water and discard peel. Cut or mash with a fork. Spread butter and cheese on top if desired (see picture).
Baked
 Use plantains that are black. Pre-heat oven at 400 F. Place whole plantain, previously rinsed and dried on baking sheet. Do not peel. Bake for 15-20 minutes. Plantain will pop out of its peel and turn light brown when it's ready (see picture).

Tostones (toas. Toah. ness.) (v)
Fried Green Plantains

Originally from Colombia and brought over to Venezuela by immigrants. Tostones are the typical snack at the beaches in Venezuela, with salad or plain.

Sometimes served as a side dish for fried fish, pabellon, and soups, double fried for best results.

*You will need a " tostonera ", it's a wooden board specially design to flatten tostones (see picture). Otherwise, use 2 small cutting boards.

Cooking time: 10 minutes

2-3 tablespoons organic extra virgin coconut oil
1 green plantain
1 teaspoon garlic paste or garlic powder
iodized sea salt

Slice off the ends of the plantain, discard and cut in half. With a knife, pull the peel off very carefully, without cutting the flesh. Remove all black spots off the flesh, if any. Cut crosswise about 1 inch thick.

Heat coconut oil in frying pan and add the plantain slices, cook for about 1 minute on each side or when it's barely turning light brown. Use paper towel to dry any excess oil. Put a slice on the tostonera, add salt and a bit of the garlic paste/powder and mash, return to heat.

Keep doing this to all the slices. Heat 1 minute on each side again. Dry in paper towel. Serve with salads, soups, fried fish, pabellon or plain.

Makes 8 tostones (1-2 portions)
1 plantain = 110 calories

*Process in the pictures is from top to bottom and from left to right

Resources

Books:
"Eating Well for Optimum Health" by: Andrew Weil, M.D.
"G I high-energy cookbook" by: Rachel Anne Hill
"Grain Brain" by: David Perlmutter, M.D.
"The Master your Metabolism cookbook" by: Jillian Michaels
"Unleash the Power of the Female Brain" by: Daniel G. Amen, M.D.
"Will Write for Food" by: Dianne Jacob

Internet:
- authoritynutrition.com
- bromectina.com
- caracasciudaddesabores.wordpress.com
- cocinaparahombres.com
- cocinayvino.com
- cocinazuliana.blogspot.com
- craigsgrapeadventure.blogspot.com
- doctoroz.com
- elfogondepolo.blogspot.com
- evamuerdelamanzana.com
- everydayhealth.com
- express.co.uk
- fitday.com
- foodandwine.com
- forvo.com
- gastronomiaenvenezuela.com
- hogarutil.com
- informe21.com
- lasrecetasdedonamartha.blogspot.com
- lasrecetasdenorellys.blogspot.com
- mis-recetas.org

- monicasancio.com
- picapica.com
- recetasgourmet.com
- rey.prensa.com
- speardiver.com
- taringa.com
- venezuelatuya.com
- wellnessmama.com
- whfoods.com
- wikipedia.com
- yogurtfromhome.com
- youtube.com

Printed in Great Britain
by Amazon.co.uk, Ltd.,
Marston Gate.